A JOHN CATT PUBLICATION

Edited by  John Tomsett

COLL

COGNITIVE
APPRENTICESHIP
IN ACTION

IN ACTION
SERIES | EDITOR
TOM
SHERRINGTON

WITH ILLUSTRATIONS BY OLIVER CAVIGLIOLI

A
WALKTHRUs
PRODUCTION

First Published 2021

by John Catt Educational Ltd,
15 Riduna Park, Station Road,
Melton, Woodbridge IP12 1QT

Tel: +44 (0) 1394 389850
Email: enquiries@johncatt.com
Website: www.johncatt.com

© **2021 John Tomsett**
Illustrations by Oliver Caviglioli

ISBN: 978 1 913622 43 5

Set and designed by John Catt Educational Limited

TABLE OF CONTENTS

SERIES FOREWORD
TOM SHERRINGTON

The idea for the *In Action* series was developed by John Catt's *Teaching WalkThrus* team after we saw how popular our *Rosenshine's Principles in Action* booklets proved to be. We realised that the same approach might support teachers to access the ideas of a range of researchers, cognitive scientists and educators. A constant challenge that we wrestle with in the world of teaching and education research is the significant distance between the formulation of a set of concepts and conclusions that might be useful to teachers and the moment when a teacher uses those ideas to teach their students in a more effective manner, thereby succeeding in securing deeper or richer learning. Sometimes so much meaning is lost along that journey, through all the communication barriers that line the road, that the implementation of the idea bears no relation to the concept its originator had in mind. Sometimes it's more powerful to hear from a teacher about how they implemented an idea than it is to read about the idea from a researcher or cognitive scientist directly – because they reduce that distance; they push some of those barriers aside.

In our *In Action* series, the authors and their collaborative partners are all teachers or school leaders close to the action in classrooms in real schools. Their strategies for translating their subjects' work into practice bring fresh energy to a powerful set of original ideas in a way that we're confident will support teachers with their professional learning and, ultimately, their classroom practice. In doing so, they are also paying their respects to the original researchers and their work. In education, as in so many walks of life, we are standing on the shoulders of giants. We believe that our selection of featured researchers and papers represents some of the most important work done in the field of education in recent times.

John Tomsett is widely known and highly regarded in the UK as the leader of a superb secondary school in York where professional learning has high status; it's embedded deeply in the school's fabric. As one of the country's first 'research schools', Huntington School has pioneered a range of approaches to support teachers in the endeavour of harnessing research to hone their craft. John has always walked the talk, leading by example, sharing his own journey as a teacher through his superb blog, conferences and leadership books. His enthusiasm for the ideas in Collins et al.'s paper was instrumental in formulating the concept of the *In Action* series and, right from the start, he wanted to give his colleagues the opportunity to share their specialist wisdom, subject by subject. The result is excellent as a book that stands alone but also makes a powerful contribution to the series as a whole.

Finally, in producing this series, we would like to acknowledge the significant influence of the researchED movement that started in 2013, run by Tom Bennett. I was present at the first conference and, having seen the movement go from strength to strength over the intervening years, I feel that many of us, including several *In Action* authors, owe a significant debt of gratitude to researchED for providing the forum where teachers' and researchers' ideas and perspectives can be shared. We are delighted, therefore, to be contributing a share of the royalties to researchED to support them in their ongoing non-profit work.

FOREWORD
PROFESSOR ALLAN COLLINS

One of the most important aspects of apprenticeship as a means of teaching is that it enables teachers to pass along tacit knowledge to learners. Because of the mass aspects of schooling, schools focus on teaching the explicit knowledge that has been accumulated in the textbooks and procedures that are taught in school. What is left out is the tacit knowledge that adults acquire over their lifetimes in solving problems and performing tasks. When adults teach by apprenticeship, they convey tacit knowledge they are hardly aware of by modelling how to do things and by coaching when they see the difficulties learners have in solving the problems and performing the tasks that the adults have been wrestling with all their lives.

This book, *Cognitive Apprenticeship in Action*, shows how teachers in different subject areas pass along their tacit knowledge to students through cognitive apprenticeships. It is a critical addition to the literature on cognitive apprenticeship, since it shows how different teachers have taken the ideas from the literature on cognitive apprenticeship and realized them in their practice. This serves to ground the theoretical ideas of cognitive apprenticeship in the actual practice of teaching in different subject areas. I am very appreciative of the efforts of the editor, John Tomsett, and the authors in making the ideas of cognitive apprenticeship come alive for teachers around the world, so that they can see what these ideas look like in actual practice.

INTRODUCTION

When I began teaching, I used to travel the 50 miles to work and back with Kate Darwin, a fellow English teacher.

Kate and I became interested specifically in the thought processes that occur between sentences. During our daily drives, we would chat about how we could make those thought processes explicit. We devised a lesson where we would take a paragraph of our own writing and insert between the paragraph's sentences our thought processes that shaped each sentence we wrote.

Our idea of articulating the thinking between sentences did not progress beyond that one-off lesson. I did not have the gumption to realise how important such thought processes are to student learning.

Little did I know that at the very same time, some 3500 miles away across the Atlantic Ocean, Allan Collins, John Seely Brown, Susan Newman and Ann Holum were developing ideas similar to those Kate and I were bandying about within the cramped confines of my Vauxhall Nova.

In 1991, Collins et al. published 'Cognitive Apprenticeship: Making Thinking Visible'. It would be nearly a quarter of a century until I encountered this paper. (And since then, it has influenced my teaching immeasurably.)

In February 2015, I was prompted to approach Alex Quigley, our erstwhile director of research, when I was faced with the following problem: my economics students' AS mock examination results were poor – the most common grade was a U.

The frustration was that *I knew they knew their economics content.* My challenge was to answer the question, *How can I train my students' thinking so that they can apply their knowledge of economics to solve the contextual problems they face in the terminal examinations?*

Alex suggested I read a certain short research paper entitled, 'Cognitive Apprenticeship: Making Thinking Visible'.

The paper identifies that 'domain (subject) knowledge ... provides insufficient clues for many students about how to actually go about solving problems and carrying out tasks in a domain. Moreover, when it is learned in isolation from realistic problem contexts and expert problem-solving practices, domain

9

knowledge tends to remain inert in situations for which it is appropriate, even for successful students.'

In order for my students to use the subject knowledge I knew they possessed, I had to teach them what Collins et al. define as 'strategic knowledge': 'the usually tacit knowledge that underlies an expert's ability to make use of concepts, facts, and procedures as necessary to solve problems and carry out tasks'.

I was the expert in the room. I knew subconsciously the skills required to apply my subject knowledge to solve an economics problem; the trouble was, I had not consciously taught my students those skills. What I had to do, according to the paper, was 'delineate the cognitive and metacognitive processes that heretofore have tacitly comprised expertise'.

I had to find a way to apply 'apprenticeship methods to largely cognitive skills'. It required 'the externalization of processes that are usually carried out internally'. Ultimately, I had to develop an apprenticeship model of teaching which made my expert thinking visible.

In response to the research paper, here is what I did: in the first lesson after the mocks, I completed the same examination paper, not answering the questions but writing on the paper what my brain would have been saying to itself, question by question, should I have attempted the paper. I did this in front of the students, live, with what I was thinking/writing projected onto the whiteboard via a visualiser.

What I wrote on the paper I insisted they wrote down verbatim on their own blank copy of the paper, a key feature of this learning experience.

The exercise showed them just how alert my brain is when I am being examined. I was teaching them, apprenticeship-style, how to *apply their domain knowledge to a new context when under pressure*. I was *making my thinking visible*.

In the second lesson after the examinations, I surprised them with a new mock paper they had not seen before. They completed the paper. The numerous students who attained a U grade first time round all improved by three or more grades.

The important thing to emphasise is that the students made these impressive gains in their examinations *without being taught any more A level Economics content*. They improved because I taught them the mental processes required to retrieve the knowledge they had learnt from their long-term memories and apply that knowledge in an efficient, precise way which answered the examination questions.

I obsess about the *golden thread* from intervention to students' outcomes. Skip a year and in the summer of 2016, those same 13 A2 Economics students surpassed themselves, attaining a grade B on average, which was 0.27 of a grade higher on average than their aspirational target grades. On the A Level Performance System (ALPS), the class performance was rated 'outstanding'.

As Collins et al. conclude, 'Ultimately, it is up to the teacher to identify ways in which cognitive apprenticeship can work in his or her own domain of teaching.'

There is no evidence-based, universal panacea to cure all teaching and learning ills. This is something Allan Collins, John Seely Brown and Ann Holum clearly knew when they published 'Cognitive Apprenticeship: Making Thinking Visible'. In their research paper, they conclude that 'cognitive apprenticeship is not a model of teaching that gives a packaged formula for instruction'. They go on to observe that, 'Ultimately, it is up to the teacher to identify ways in which cognitive apprenticeship can work in his or her own domain of teaching.'

This book, *Cognitive Apprenticeship In Action*, gives a sharp, detailed account of how the classroom practice of 23 teachers from one school has been influenced by the principles of Collins et al.'s 'Cognitive Apprenticeship'. Not one teacher has adopted cognitive apprenticeship as a complete 'packaged formula'; all the teachers have identified aspects of cognitive apprenticeship which help make visible the expert thinking in their 'own domain of teaching'.

'Cognitive Apprenticeship: Making Thinking Visible'

Before you read any further, it is essential to give you a brief overview of the key principles of cognitive apprenticeship espoused in the original paper published in 1991. Collins et al. took the traditional apprenticeship method – modelling, scaffolding, fading, coaching – and applied it to schooling. They focused particularly upon making the implicit explicit, upon articulating aloud the unspoken. The very thing that attracted me about cognitive apprenticeship was how it is 'a model of instruction that works to make thinking visible'.

The principles for designing cognitive apprenticeship environments as conceived by Collins et al. are expressed within a 'framework consisting of four dimensions that constitute any learning environment: content, method, sequence, and sociology'. The characteristics of each dimension are outlined below:

CONTENT: types of knowledge required for expertise

The fact that Collins et al. begin with content is important, because without knowledge there is no learning. ***Domain knowledge*** is where they start, but as they also point out, whilst it is 'important, [it] provides insufficient clues for many students about how to solve problems and accomplish tasks in a domain'. *Heuristics*, or 'tricks of the trade' as Collins et al. describe them, 'are generally effective techniques and approaches for accomplishing tasks' and provide a good starting point for addressing a challenge. So you know your domain knowledge, and heuristics help apply that knowledge, but when heuristics do not work, you require *control strategies*, or what we might call metacognitive skills, which help you think through different approaches to a challenge beyond the limited effectiveness of heuristics. Finally, within this first dimension, you need to know different ways of *learning* any of these previous three types of knowledge.

METHOD: ways to promote the development of expertise

For 'method' read 'methods of teaching'. Here Collins et al. outline six elements of apprenticeship-style teaching, beginning with the teacher *modelling* a task or process and the students observing. *Scaffolding* support helps the students complete a task. Next, the teacher observes the student whilst *coaching* them to complete the task. The next stage of the teaching methods process is for students to *articulate* what they know and how they think when they complete the task. When the task is complete, teachers show students how to *reflect* upon their performance and compare it with the performance of others. The final method stage is to ask students to identify and then solve their own problems; the level of teacher guidance is faded and the tasks allow greater student *exploration*.

SEQUENCING: keys to ordering learning activities

When it comes to sequencing activities, Collins et al. insist that you *begin globally* before looking at local skills. This gives the learner a 'conceptual map … before attending to the details of the terrain'. Tasks must be sequenced to ensure an *increase in complexity* and then teachers must *diversify* tasks, to help students explore the breadth and depth of the subject domain.

SOCIOLOGY: social characteristics of learning environments

The fourth and final dimension begins with ensuring the learning is 'situated', where students 'carry out tasks and solve problems in an environment that reflects the multiple uses to which their knowledge will be put in the future'. According to Collins et al., *situated learning* encourages students to use their knowledge actively, rather than just passively receive it, so they can see the purpose of their learning. They then encourage the development of *communities of practice* where students find an intrinsic motivation for their learning which goes beyond pleasing teachers or gaining examination grades, and where the students *exploit cooperation* between each other to enhance the community's learning as a whole.

Collins et al. provide this useful summary of the four dimensions:

PRINCIPLES FOR DESIGNING
COGNITIVE APPRENTICESHIP ENVIRONMENTS

CONTENT: types of knowledge required for expertise

- **Domain knowledge:** subject matter specific concepts, facts, and procedures

- **Heuristic strategies:** generally applicable techniques for accomplishing tasks

- **Control strategies:** general approaches for directing one's solution process

- **Learning strategies:** knowledge about how to learn new concepts, facts, and procedures

METHOD: ways to promote the development of expertise

- **Modeling:** teacher performs a task so students can observe

- **Coaching:** teacher observes and facilitates while students perform a task

- **Scaffolding:** teacher provides supports to help the student perform a task

- **Articulation:** teacher encourages students to verbalize their knowledge and thinking

- **Reflection:** teacher enables students to compare their performance with others

- **Exploration:** teacher invites students to pose and solve their own problems

SEQUENCING: keys to ordering learning activities

- **Global before local skills:** focus on conceptualizing the whole task before executing the parts

- **Increasing complexity:** meaningful tasks gradually increasing in difficulty

- **Increasing diversity:** practice in a variety of situations to emphasize broad application

---

> **SOCIOLOGY: social characteristics of learning environments**
>
> - **Situated learning:** students learn in the context of working on realistic tasks
>
> - **Community of practice:** communication about different ways to accomplish meaningful tasks
>
> - **Intrinsic motivation:** students set personal goals to seek skills and solutions
>
> - **Cooperation:** students work together to accomplish their goals

Collins et al. focused upon the cognitive apprenticeship teaching processes required to make thinking visible to students in reading, writing and mathematical problem-solving. When I first came to cognitive apprenticeship, I focused upon the metacognitive processes required to answer A level Economics examination questions, the general types of reasoning that help you apply your subject knowledge to tackle academic tasks. What has come to interest me as much, however, having worked with Collins et al.'s ideas for many years, is defining the expert thinking processes for each subject in the curriculum. *What is it to think like an expert physicist or chef or musician?*

So, when I introduced my Huntington colleagues to the original 'Cognitive Apprenticeship' paper and challenged them to identify the unique expert thinking processes in their individual subjects and to describe how they make those thinking processes visible, it was a hugely provocative question. Some found it especially hard to pinpoint an answer. Crucially, my challenge sparked their intellectual curiosity, so that when I suggested we write a book about the influence of cognitive apprenticeship on our practice, I was overwhelmed by positive responses.

I set my expert colleagues the task of writing a short essay which explained how certain principles of cognitive apprenticeship as defined by Collins et al. had helped them improve their teaching and their students' learning. I wanted them to explain specifically how they had made their subjects' thinking processes visible to students.

When it came to identifying the unique expert thinking processes in their individual subjects, their answers were rooted in domain knowledge. Unique expert thinking processes and content are inextricably linked. And the examples of fundamental thinking/content for each subject are predictably both

14

subjective and partial. You may well disagree with their selections – in fact, *we expect that you will and welcome that challenge.*

Furthermore, as each chapter has been written by a teacher at Huntington School, the chapters do not follow a set structure. Each writer had the liberty to write about the thinking processes germane to his or her subject in a way s/he felt appropriate.

Cognitive apprenticeship: an evidence review

Jane Elsworth

Cognitive apprenticeship is an approach that emphasises the importance of the process in which a master of a skill teaches that skill to an apprentice. Observing schooling methods and studying these constructivist approaches to human learning led to the development of the theory of cognitive apprenticeship proposed by Collins et al. (1989). In this paper, they cite several successful studies that embody the basic methods of cognitive apprenticeship focused on improving reading, writing and mathematics.

The first such study is Palincsar and Brown's (1984) reciprocal teaching of reading technique that models and coaches students in four strategic skills to support those who can decode but have poor reading comprehension. This technique has proved to be very effective at raising students' scores on reading tests in a range of studies undertaken in the USA. It has been used widely in other English-speaking countries but is less common in the UK. There is some evidence of promise from previous evaluations of reciprocal teaching, including a meta-analysis of 16 studies, which showed an average impact equivalent to around four months' additional progress. In the UK, recent evaluations of programmes that have included a focus on teaching reading comprehension strategies have not found such an extensive impact. For example, the Education Endowment Foundation (EEF) evaluation of the Reciprocal Reading programme (O'Hare et al., 2019), a trial comprising over 5000 KS2 pupils in 98 schools across the UK, found on average an impact equivalent to around two months of additional progress in both their overall reading and reading comprehension.

The second example is an approach to the teaching of writing that relies on cognitive apprenticeship from Scardamalia and Bereiter (1983, 1984 and 1985). This approach provides explicit procedural supports, through a combination of modelling, coaching, scaffolding and fading in the form

---

of prompts. These are aimed at helping students adopt more sophisticated writing strategies. In a series of studies by the authors in 1985, procedural facilitations were developed to help elementary school students in the USA evaluate, diagnose and decide on revisions for their compositions. Results showed that each type was effective, independent of the other supports. And when all were combined, they resulted in superior revisions for nearly every student.

Indeed, research by Graham et al. (2016) identified 11 studies that examined interventions related to teaching writing strategies to students and/or using a 'model-practise-reflect' instructional cycle. All of the studies found positive effects on at least one writing outcome, including outcomes in the overall writing quality, genre elements, organisation, word choice, writing output, and writing process domains. Additionally, the EEF guidance report *Improving Literacy in Secondary Schools* (Quigley and Coleman, 2019) suggests the breaking-down of complex writing tasks through the use of explicit instruction, scaffolding and modelling by teachers of planning, monitoring and evaluation. This is echoed in 'Principles of Instruction' by Barak Rosenshine (2012), which is based on cognitive science, observational studies of 'master teachers' and studies that tested the learning strategies with students. It is particularly resonant in the first of the four strands – 'Sequencing concepts and modelling' – identified by Tom Sherrington in *Rosenshine's Principles in Action* (2019).

Cognitive apprenticeship has many elements of what has been more recently called 'metacognition and self-regulation' by the EEF in their *Metacognition and Self-Regulated Learning* guidance report (Quigley et al., 2018) and is rated by the EEF as 'high impact for very low cost, based on extensive evidence'. Their guidance report, based on the evidence review by Muijs and Bokhove (2020) quotes a range of studies that have shown that self-regulated learning and, in particular, metacognition have a significant impact on pupils' academic performance, beyond that predicted by prior achievement. There is some evidence to suggest that disadvantaged pupils are less likely to use such strategies and are therefore more likely to benefit from the whole range of approaches to supporting metacognitive and self-regulatory skills, including explicit teaching. Recommendation 2 of the guidance report states that 'particular strategies are often quite subject- or task-specific, and the evidence suggests that they are best taught through subject content'. Recommendation 3 states that 'to move from novice to expert, our pupils need to know how an expert athlete, artist, historian, or scientist habitually thinks and acts. We need to make these largely implicit processes explicit to our novice learners' (Quigley et al., 2018).

So, cognitive apprenticeship has an impressive heritage. Collins et al.'s paper published in 1991 is Janus-faced in that it brought together a number of pieces of research around metacognitive practice that had emerged over the previous decade or more (Flavell famously coined the phrase 'metacognition' in 1976) and then acted as a springboard for 30 years of development of metacognitive practice in the classroom. Publications such as the EEF's *Metacognition and Self-Regulated Learning* guidance report have deep roots.

When it comes to making thinking visible, there are three main threads running through the chapters:

1. The individual chapter author's notion of what constitutes expert thinking in his or her subject specialism;

2. How you make that subject specialist thinking visible to students;

3. How you make visible the thinking required to apply expert knowledge and understanding to problem-solving.

I have organised the chapters into four sections, reflecting the four dimensions of cognitive apprenticeship environments. There is a significant focus upon the content and method dimensions, whilst my colleagues have articulated promising analysis of sequencing and sociology. All the contributions explore more than one dimension and several cover all four.

Over the years I have worked with a number of subject departments; consequently, I know that consensus amongst teachers is a rare – and, arguably, undesirable – thing. Debating the curriculum with your colleagues is at the heart of curriculum development. If this book provokes creative discussions amongst your colleagues about what and how you teach, then it will have served its purpose.

My colleagues have *wilful humility*: they are determined practitioners who want to be as good as they can be and accept that we can all improve our practice. Thus, the intention of this book is to stimulate debate, rather than claim to be definitive.

It is a privilege to work at Huntington School. The level of teacher learning is phenomenal. Dylan Wiliam described our teacher learning programme as 'the most complete and compelling vision that I have seen for a school that places teacher learning at the heart of its endeavours, rather than being bolted on as an afterthought' (Tomsett and Uttley, 2020).

What follows is the fruit of that Huntington vision, as my brilliant colleagues make their own pedagogic thinking visible, using the cognitive apprenticeship model articulated by Collins et al. over 30 years ago.

We know and hope you will want to debate some of what you read here. If you would like to engage with our curriculum development team, please contact us at Huntington; indeed, *informed debate is the fuel of curriculum development.*

It has been a huge pleasure working with my colleagues at Huntington School in realising *Cognitive Apprenticeship In Action.* I have learnt a huge amount about each subject and, as a headteacher, I have a better grasp of the school curriculum than I have ever had. Better late than never.

When I challenged my colleagues to think hard about their subject disciplines, they responded with genuine zeal. We had some tremendous discussions about their subjects. They met every deadline I asked of them, whilst teaching during the coronavirus pandemic; indeed, the only one of us to miss any deadlines was me. And without their courage to publish their work, there would have been no book. They are, to a person, heroes.

I set out in 1988 as a green teacher of English literature, full of *Dead Poets Society* idealism. I had an inkling that teaching students how to think like an expert writer was *a thing*, but did not have the conceptual framework to make that real until I discovered the work of Collins et al., some 25 years later. Since then, I have worked for several years to develop my cognitive apprenticeship skills in my teaching, tweaking what I do year after year so that I make my expert thinking visible in economics and, occasionally still, in my beloved English.

I am a better teacher now, at the end of my career, than I have ever been. And that is down, primarily, to the work of Professor Allan Collins, John Seely Brown and Ann Holum, to whom I am deeply grateful.

The one other person I want to thank is Tom Sherrington, series editor, co-conspirator and dear friend. Tom has been an inspiration to me, and working with him these past few years, when we have both faced adversity, has been life-enhancing. I owe him more than he might ever know.

John Tomsett, January 2021

A note about referencing

As you might imagine, the paper is referred to throughout this book. While we have reproduced the paper in full as an appendix, we have not referenced it in a traditional way; rather, we hope that quotations from 'Cognitive Apprenticeship: Making Thinking Visible' will tempt you to read the paper yourself. Doing so will certainly give you a deeper understanding of how and why the paper's principles have so influenced one school's classroom practice.

CONTENT
Types of knowledge required for expertise

The fact that Collins et al. begin with content is important, because without knowledge there is no learning. ***Domain knowledge*** is where they start, but as they also point out, whilst it is 'important, [it] provides insufficient clues for many students about how to solve problems and accomplish tasks in a domain'. ***Heuristics***, or 'tricks of the trade' as Collins et al. describe them, 'are generally effective techniques and approaches for accomplishing tasks' and provide a good starting point for addressing a challenge. So you know your domain knowledge and heuristics help apply that knowledge, but when heuristics do not work, you require ***control strategies***, or what we might call metacognitive skills, which help you think through different approaches to a challenge beyond the limited effectiveness of heuristics. Finally, within this first dimension, you need to know different ways of ***learning*** any of these previous three types of knowledge.

CONTENT
Types of knowledge required for expertise

DOMAIN KNOWLEDGE
Subject matter specific concepts,
facts, and procedures

HEURISTIC STRATEGIES
Generally applicable techniques
for accomplishing tasks

CONTROL STRATEGIES
General approaches for directing
one's solution process

LEARNING STRATEGIES
Knowledge about how to learn new
concepts, facts, and procedures

A summary introduction to Dimension One:
CONTENT

Matt Savory's chapter on thinking like a biologist is a perfect place to begin our exploration of cognitive apprenticeship *in action*. Matt illustrates how all four of Collins et al.'s dimensions combine. He outlines how 'the most important strategic knowledge that must be developed in biology is the scale within which the various concepts and ideas of the subject must fit'. He explains the methods he uses to teach this knowledge, how he situates the knowledge in global terms before he drills down into the local, and finishes with the phrase, a 'new generation of biologists', which reflects the sense of cooperation and community which is the hallmark of his biology classes.

Hugh Richards is an ardent historian. He is a dedicated member of the Historical Association and has that brilliant capacity to develop curriculum leadership in younger members of his department. According to Hugh, 'expert historians don't merely have opinions; they construct arguments based on the strongest evidence they can muster', and whilst he talks a lot about teaching methods, at the heart of what he is teaching are the cognitive control strategies which characterise his subject's domain knowledge.

From the very beginning of their Huntington musical career, students are treated as musicians. 'At Huntington, we teach every lesson through sound,' explains Liz Dunbar, our expert subject leader of music, for whom domain knowledge is all. In her chapter, she explains the bookends of a Huntington musical education. Our youngest begin with exploring ostinato and seven years later are composing in a community of performers where teachers are co-constructors of music who 'need to be ready to experiment … to be ready to fail, and have countless false starts'.

According to Tom Norris, 'an expert physicist should be able to look at almost any physical situation and identify the *essence* of what is happening, in terms of the underpinning physical mechanisms'. He explains the several teaching methods he employs to enable students to 'identify the *essential* physical features of the given situation … and then *codify* the essential features of the situation to produce an accurate physics representation/model'. Tom shows how to bridge the gap between domain knowledge and student learning through metacognitive teaching processes.

Finally in this section, the assistant headteacher in charge of science, Beth Hartwell, reminds us of the interconnectivity of the three science disciplines, and how 'the links between the disciplines are explicitly taught to ensure that our students have a holistic approach to their practice'. Beth's contribution again covers more than one dimension, but at its heart is developing students' mastery of scientific domain knowledge in its broadest sense.

BIOLOGY

BY MATT SAVORY

As humans, we are encouraged to think about the wonder of nature and how it works from a very young age. We build schema that enable us to interact successfully with our environment. Consequently, the first challenge for a biology teacher is to ascertain exactly what our pupils think they already understand about their world. Early experiences shape our intrinsic motivation for studying the subject and some of the best biologists are those who are happy to re-evaluate what they think they know, which ultimately depends upon how willing they are to evolve from any original preconceptions. Such an attitude to learning biology allows students to make progress through the synthesis of new links between different biological contexts.

Biology as a subject can be classified into the key strands (or 'big ideas') from 'Best Evidence Science Teaching (BEST)' (Salters' Institute, 2018):

- The cellular basis of life
- Heredity and life cycles
- Organisms and their environments
- Variation, adaptation and evolution
- Health and disease

The research from BEST also encourages the consideration of content (including the importance of vocabulary), competencies and concepts. To weave these together would allow biology students to apply the core principles of the subject to unfamiliar situations and approach these in the same way that an 'expert' or 'career' biologist would. For those students who might suggest they don't need biology as part of their preparation for life, it could be worth referencing situations such as a pandemic, where even a basic level of scientific literacy would enable an individual to make informed choices when faced with evidence in the media and from public health organisations. Emphasising how the choices made in light of the evidence can affect both individuals around us and our wider society is a compelling argument for the importance of using biology in context.

Among the most important strategic knowledge that must be developed in biology is the scale within which the various concepts and ideas of the subject must fit. Students must be able to see biology as a lens on familiar organisms, from their cells to their tissues, then building up to organs and organ systems, followed by a consideration of the whole organism and its place and interactions within an ecosystem. It would then be possible to see how these ecosystems come together to form our world as we know it, with all of these organisational hierarchies also being underpinned by the movement of molecules at the nanoscale. In biology, we are constantly exploring the relationship between the nano, the micro, the meso, the macro and the supra.

Cognitive apprenticeship allows students to see the 'processes of work' and takes the time to 'make thinking visible', which can be facilitated in biology when getting students to internalise a sense of scale. Both modelling and the use of models are essential for understanding complex ideas such as mass transport in plants or the contraction of a muscle fibre. The content can be taught through expert teacher explanation followed by the creation of physical models to represent the changes at a molecular level. Some scaffolding will be required for students to successfully engage with the model making process, such as a set of questions for consideration, or evaluation of a pre-existing model.

The teacher can also circulate and participate in coaching conversations to offer refinements to the model, with similar conversations perhaps already taking place peer to peer if students are working in a small group. An extension to this strategy could be to pause the rest of the class and get them to listen in on just one of the group conversations, offering peer critique of the level of understanding shown, which allows for fading of teacher support and coaching over time. As Collins et al. point out, 'The teacher's thinking must be made visible to the students and the student's thinking must be made visible to the teacher,' a notion central to the success of the cognitive apprenticeship approach.

These student-created models not only contribute to the understanding of biological scale but can assist with more confident articulation of the concept represented. They also provide an opportunity for reflection on the suitability of the model and exploration of how a better model could be developed. Through this approach, the processes of building a scientific model have been identified and made visible, thus allowing students to return to these processes when reviewing the content or when attempting application of the concept in an unfamiliar or examination context.

Cognitive apprenticeship considers sequencing to be a key skill and recognises increasing complexity and diversity within a learning environment. This sits alongside the advice given in biology examination specifications that the least complex ideas should be the starting point and then the concept can be built upon from there. Whilst this makes good sense in terms of sequencing, starting teaching from a cellular level has its challenges. Just because something is small doesn't necessarily mean it is easy to understand, and in fact the more you zoom in when looking through the lens of biology, the less tangible the ideas become for students. They will have seen whole ecosystems and organisms, and can probably extend their thinking to organ systems, organs and cells, but a concept such as the functions of individual organelles and the interplay between these tiny structures can lead to a detachment from the bigger picture.

It is important to remember Collins et al.'s simple principle 'Global before local'. It is the role of the teacher to continuously return the mind of the student to something they can visualise on the biological scale – again, a reason why the use of models can be beneficial. By returning to this, the teacher can situate an 'abstract task in an authentic context' and emphasise the relevance of the work being done.

At the beginning of teaching the first A level topic on cells, I introduce the idea of scale being fundamental to the study of biology. I give the students ten images of objects ranging from subatomic particles up to an organism. As the expert biologist, I do not see them as simply ten independent objects, as a novice might, but as items whose properties are also important when you consider the interaction between each layer of the hierarchy. However, I also know that if students cannot relate the objects together in terms of magnitude, there will be a limit to their understanding of the interrelation between these complex properties. For example, polar molecules cannot cross a cell membrane despite some being small enough to do so because of the interaction of this polarity with the molecules that the membrane is composed of. An understanding of scale alone here might result in students suggesting the molecules could pass through the membrane; however, linking together the concept of scale with molecular properties would allow the student to reach the correct understanding of the concept of membrane permeability.

The task is to put these ten objects into order of magnitude from the image and students' pre-existing knowledge. At this point, common misconceptions are often revealed and addressed. Once they have done this, I would model sorting the images myself and attribute them to a continuum of scale or measurement. Statements such as 'proteins must be smaller than cells as the cells are made of proteins' make my reasoning explicit and discrepancies between my ordering and theirs would be highlighted and discussed in order to ensure that any misconceptions do not still stand. This helps students to integrate their prior knowledge and lays the ground for attributing new learning about objects and their interactions to this scale.

The next time we approach a new topic, in order to get them to develop their expertise, I ask students to repeat the task but now with objects specific to the current topic. If learning about the kidney, for example, I would get them to sort the following: kidney, sodium ion, nephron, molecule of ADH, basement membrane, aquaporin. I scaffold this by referring back to the original sorting activity: 'What approach did we take then? How did this approach help us to appreciate scale in biology?' They are encouraged to articulate their thinking to me and to each other through coaching questions such as, 'Why is it that sodium ions are not able to move across the cell membranes, as you have said that they are small enough to do so?' This style of questioning gets them to reflect upon their ideas of scale but also links them to the properties of the objects that they are sorting. We can then reflect as a class upon whether they have made the right choices and justifications. Finally, this thinking can be applied to the learning of new concepts with further independent student exploration. By the end of year 13, students will have applied this expert thinking not only to the kidney but also to gene expression, control of blood glucose levels, succession in an ecosystem and many other biological objects and processes.

Over time, students will come across a hugely diverse set of ideas within biology, from epigenetics and subsequent behavioural influences to the Calvin cycle in the process of photosynthesis. The ability to then recognise the interconnectivity between these concepts and the movement between different levels of complexity during discussion is integral to the development of strong schemas. Equally vital is a strong sense of scale and an ability to use this alongside physical models of the concepts. To be able to witness the lightbulb moment when all of the concepts come together is one of the great privileges we have as teachers, and we would hope that encouraging students to highlight commonality and develop subject-specific transferable skills would facilitate the creation of a new generation of biologists.

HISTORY

BY HUGH RICHARDS

In terms of school history, understanding questions and deciding how to organise responses are the most important moments in a history examination. Sometimes, students emerge from the examination room and explain that although they have some rock-solid knowledge of the past, they were simply unable to answer the questions. Often, faced with the solitariness of the examination, our more vulnerable learners' final scripts reveal one of four types of examination essay disaster:

1. No response written at all

2. A few attempts at the start of the paper which are angrily crossed out

3. Responses that answer the question but fail to use sufficient historical knowledge

4. Responses incorporating strong knowledge but which don't address the question

Understanding the process of structuring historical writing is fundamental to how academic historians work. Expert historians don't merely have opinions; they construct arguments based on the strongest evidence they can muster. To do this, they use written argument to marshal their thinking, organise evidence, construct more robust and meaningful history and, ultimately, communicate with each other.

Diana Laffin explains, however, that there is a 'gulf … between the history that students write and the history that historians write' (Laffin, 2013). Professional historians very rarely write in the form of a short essay, yet the short essay is a common medium used by student historians to present the outcome of their process of enquiry. These single-sentence, high-value questions require students to select and deploy appropriate knowledge effectively – whilst avoiding irrelevant issues – throughout a coherent and clearly argued extended response.

These essay questions provide only a very few, relatively subtle signposts to direct the student's thinking. The instant a student begins to process such questions is often the make-or-break moment. Misinterpret the wording of the question and the subsequent extended answer may not be credited at all. Therefore, at Huntington, we began to explore how to help students approach this complex cognitive process in stages, aided by a visual system of organisation that they create for themselves without any extra prompting. We eventually settled on a technique we call 'spiderplanning'.

The spiderplanning process

1. The process begins with a circle, drawn on a blank piece of paper. Inside that circle, students put the focus of the question into their own words. Creating a circle to fill helps them interrogate the question. At this stage they also ask themselves, 'What mistakes might I make?' This question helps them reflect on previous learning, feedback and the errors they have made with a given type of question.

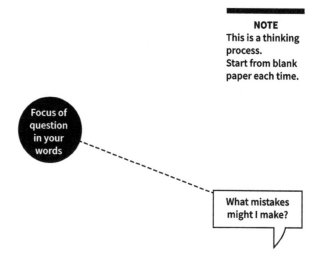

2. Stage 2 asks students to add the four major points they would make to answer the question. They can also make a judgement here to help them get into the habit of creating well-argued writing, which is crucial when we develop spiderplanning skills further at A level.

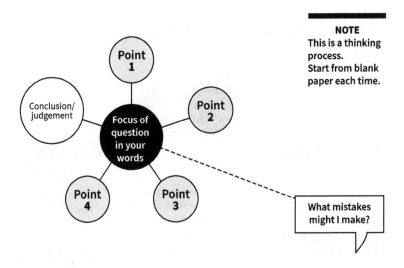

3. Students then select facts and examples that prove the points they have chosen to make and add these as another layer outside each point.

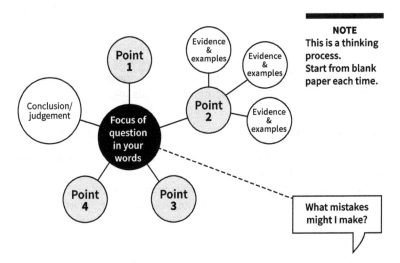

4. Finally, students then use the plan whilst they write, jotting down anything more they want to remember and ticking off what they have done, to retain the structure and focus on the question.

Here is a worked example, based on the following GCSE essay question: *'Hitler's position of total power by August 1934 was achieved mainly through the use of violence.' How far do you agree with this view?*

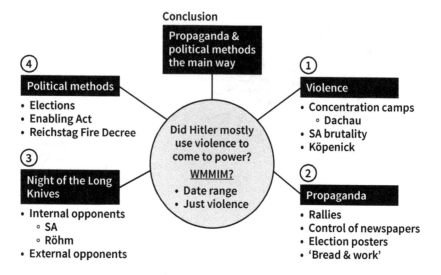

Crucially, as we develop students' use of spiderplans, we constantly re-emphasise the inherent qualities of expert historical writing that drive it: splitting a question into analytical parts, making a well-judged claim, using evidence to support that claim, before bringing the threads together into an overall final judgement.

There are two crucial cognitive apprenticeship features of the process.

Firstly, the creation of the diagram is crucial as the process makes the students explore the processes they need to work through before they start to write. Clearly, this process has been informed by more than just the idea of cognitive apprenticeship – notably the work of Christodoulou on deliberate practice (2017) and Caviglioli on dual coding (2019) – but it has the principles of cognitive apprenticeship at its heart.

Critically, we always start from a blank piece of paper, and the students draw their own diagram. As such, they are engaging with the thought process in a way that is always replicable in the exam situation – there is no 'fading' necessary in terms of resources, only in terms of teacher support. The table below shows how students are introduced to spiderplanning over a 20-lesson GCSE unit:

Modelling	Spiderplanning is explicitly taught as an empty template before the teacher immediately models one example. The teacher's internal thinking is communicated via a *running commentary*. In the first few attempts, students' spiderplans are comparatively discussed as a class to expose stronger and weaker elements.
Scaffolding	Students are asked to memorise the strategy, before completing several spiderplans over a sequence of lessons as guided practice with the teacher. Whole-class discussions continue, as detailed below.
Fading	Increasingly independent practice is embarked upon towards the end of the 20-lesson sequence, coupled with more development into full writtten answers.

Secondly, teachers get an opportunity to see the planning and can intervene, compare, discuss and expose the cognitive processes at work. A vital element here is giving some time to allow students to expose their thought processes in a way teachers can understand. As a result, perhaps the most important stage is the scaffolding one. A class of students faced with the same question will always use a range of structures and paragraph topics. Regularly comparing this diversity of structures and content and guiding the class to evaluate stronger and weaker structures allows the thought processes to be surfaced. In our experience, students learn a great deal by comparing their own thinking to other answers. As Collins et al. point out, it is crucial that 'students assume the dual roles of producer and critic'.

One opportunity for responsive teaching and timely intervention is illustrated below, showing how this might look in a lesson. Once students have drafted their own spiderplan in response to the question, the four major points that each student has chosen can be discussed in a comparative way on the whiteboard, thus:

Hitler's position of total power by August 1934 was achieved mainly through the use of violence. **How far do you agree with this view?**

STUDENT A	STUDENT B	STUDENT C	STUDENT D
1 Night of the Long Knives	1 Night of the Long Knives	1 1920s	1 Political methods
2 Enabling Act	2 Camps	2 1928-32	2 Propaganda
3 Reichstag Fire	3 Gestapo	3 1932-33	3 Violence
4 Propaganda	4 SA violence	4 1934	4 Night of the Long Knives

Key points that would emerge from comparative classroom discussion of these structures:

- Students A and D would both address the question well. It's useful to expose that there are multiple routes to a valid answer.

- Student B has misunderstood the scope of the question and only focused on violent methods. Highlighting this helps with future 'What mistakes might I make?' phases.

- Student C will perhaps struggle to compare violence with other methods. It is a valid approach but very susceptible to sliding into narrative rather than comparative analysis.

Following this discussion, the class chooses a structure to plan collaboratively in more detail. Even with no follow-up task, this process is powerful, allowing deliberate practice of those crucial moments after first reading an essay question. If students do draft in full, the spiderplan process results in much less misdirected effort. Students B and C would not only write better work but also understand why it was stronger than what they had initially planned. Crucially, when we compare and contrast different spiderplans, 'such comparisons provide the basis for diagnosing student difficulties and for making incremental adjustments in student performance'.

When students complete a full essay alone, for example in a mock examination, the spiderplan is hugely helpful to the teacher. Students who have written a poor-quality essay but have spiderplanned before writing give their teacher a chance to trace their thinking, and understand where the problems have occurred, instead of trying to unpick a finished essay. If the problem is found in the central circle, work needs to be done on the comprehension of questions. If the outer ring of evidence is patchy, the student may have interpreted the question perfectly but needs a more secure knowledge base.

Although we use different combinations of metacognition and dual coding for A level and KS3, the most successful ones we have used so far tend to follow these principles:

RECOMMENDATIONS

Think carefully about all the knowledge, skills and processes required by a huge summative task. Teach these by weaving them into ordinary lessons.

Make this a visual, diagrammatic process that builds a piece of the thinking at each stage.

Develop distinctly different visual planning organisers for different types of exam question.

Don't print – ever! Ensure they always practise from a blank sheet of paper, using the process of drawing to structure the thinking.

Show your working whenever you can: **expose the thought process** when you plan essay structures with them.

Encourage students to ask themselves *'What mistakes might I make?'* and discuss these each time you think about a question or plan a response as a class.

This combination of diagrammatic planning and metacognition to help students marshal their historical thinking is pure cognitive apprenticeship. In our teaching, we model the principles of cognitive apprenticeship at each and every stage. We take no shortcuts. We work as hard as the students need to in order to make our expert thinking visible.

MUSIC

BY LIZ DUNBAR

At Huntington, we work with students from the full range of socioeconomic backgrounds. When they arrive in year 7, some students have already had seven years of one-to-one expert instrumental tuition, while others haven't had any music education at all. All our teaching is mixed ability, so the National Youth Orchestra violinist learns side by side with the student who hasn't even experienced classroom singing at primary school.

So, how do we teach the creative process of composition to such a diverse student body?

Teaching students 'how' music works immediately levels the playing field. It's interesting how students who don't see themselves as musicians can respond to composition and improvisation tasks just as imaginatively as those who have had formal instrumental training.

Music teachers have to make their thinking visible through sound. Yes, there are words; yes, you can draw pictures and diagrams; yes, you can make analogies; but ultimately, students have to be able to understand your teaching points in sound, and be able to make, develop and refine their ideas in sound.

Learning how to hear like a musician is intellectually challenging. Learning how to create, shape and refine ideas in sound is harder again. As a result, you have to begin this process by taking the smallest steps and repeating and reinforcing at every stage.

Here is an account of the first steps we take with all of our mixed prior attainment classes of 30 students. This is how they begin to discover the craft of creating original musical ideas for themselves.

Through this process, we explore how aspects of the cognitive apprenticeship model (modelling, scaffolding, coaching and fading) can be used to develop students' abilities to craft and manipulate musical ideas successfully. It goes without saying that built into this process is time to fail, and time to create through pure exploration.

Early in the first half term, we get everyone in year 7 responding in sound through live music-making. We start with the ostinato. It is a commonly employed compositional device based on the simple notion of the repetition of something memorable. It is a device that has no historical or cultural boundaries, so it is relevant to everyone. It can be as simple or as complicated as you like, and, with a little experience, it can be layered with other ostinati with immediately satisfying results.

At Huntington, we teach every lesson through sound. We treat everyone as a musician. We make every task accessible so that everyone can produce a 'musical' response regardless of their previous experience. So, in the first lesson, we begin by isolating and **modelling** a single ostinato layer in sound. Students watch and hear the teacher provide both accessible and challenging musical models, and each model is described and explained using specialist musical language. Then students get stuck in and start recreating the model for themselves. As they play and laugh, and grapple with the challenge, they also start to articulate what they are doing with fragments of musical language.

Here's what the ostinato looks like in notation, though of course we teach through sound first and foremost to make the task universally accessible. It's an ostinato with personality. It's syncopated and has a natural groove making it immediately appealing. Most importantly, it's playable by everyone in the room.

We only explore what the notation version tells us once we have established an aural model. For some students, this may be the first thing they have ever played and responded to in live sound. The student sees and hears a musical idea come alive in their hands. They are recreating a real fragment of something they have heard before, but most likely have never thought about or understood. It's a really powerful moment.

The teacher then presents a second ostinato which has many things in common with the first. The similarities and differences between the two ideas is, in effect, the **scaffold**. We now leave exploration and thinking time to allow the students to work out that the two ostinati fit together, alongside two questions: 'What do the two ideas have in common? What makes them different to one another?'

This learning through discovery is the springboard into a discussion on why these two ideas work so well together. We examine what the musical material is made of and start to build a vocabulary to enable students to describe what's going on.

In the next lesson, students create their own ostinato, now that they have a model. Here you **fade** your support as the students gain confidence. Much of what they produce is derivative, of course, but it's the first step for many in believing that they can create something which has the potential to be good.

This first ever re-creative and creative task is accessible, memorable, rewarding, with component parts deliberately brought into the foreground. It is equitable, with each student, no matter their background or experience, able to learn the fundamentals of composition and experience musical success.

Six years on, and students at A level are equipped with a tool kit of compositional devices, and invaluable hands-on experience of the craft. At this level, the demands of composition require students to demonstrate a 'balance of unity and variety' in their work. This can be achieved in a variety of ways, for example in a student's handling of modulation in harmony. To begin with, we explore this area through established models. When harmonising melodies in Bach stylistics exercises, we establish a little mantra: 'Can I go V–I? If I can't go V–I, can I go to V? If I can't go to V, I'm in the wrong key.' It works in this context.

The problem is, it commonly sounds formulaic when applied to students' work. You can see the ropes and pulleys as it were. So how do you make the process of creating a more sophisticated kind of modulation 'visible' to the students so they can use it, yet invisible or barely visible to the listener? You begin by isolating a simple example of modulation in sound and demonstrate/explain how it works. Then you present it in context to show how the music arrives at this point and then moves beyond it. You repeat the process with a slightly more complicated example, isolated, explained and put in context. You continue this process until you reach the harder to hear, and more subtle examples.

Equipped with this aural training and experience, students then go in search of a modulation, the more remote and remarkable the better. They return with a challenge for you. Live, unprepared, you take apart their chosen modulation. Let them hear and see you work out the pitches involved, sounding out and verbalising your thinking as you decipher exactly what's going on until you've cracked the code. Consider Faure's 'Requiem, the Agnus Dei', which takes the tonic and modulates remotely, becoming the flattened submediant's mediant. Genius. Glorious. Breathtaking.

Now that you've demonstrated that process, students have a way of working that enables them to tease out the component parts of the harmony and chords and their relationship to one another, and they can bring that process into the explorations of their own compositional ideas.

It's really important that you don't just present pre-prepared examples. Dare to fail, so that students can see that it is hard work, that it takes time to hone the skills. As a teacher, you need to be ready to experiment, you need to be ready to fail, and have countless false starts. Work through it in sound together. The learning comes from the experimentation, the struggle, the reworking, the frustrations and triumphs of the creative process, all founded upon the knowledge and thinking made visible in that first teacher-led lesson.

By using methods derived from cognitive apprenticeship in analysis and composition, by bringing the cognitive process by which things are made into full view, we make expert disciplinary thinking visible and accessible.

MAKING THINKING VISIBLE IN...

PHYSICS

BY TOM NORRIS

The core ideas of physics are supposed to be *fundamental* and *universal*. This means that an expert physicist should be able to look at almost any physical situation and identify the essence of what is happening in terms of the underpinning physical mechanisms. This ability is assessed in higher-level physics exams, where students can be presented with absolutely any physical situation to analyse: from the everyday (e.g. simply lifting an object or pushing a shopping trolley) to the less familiar (e.g. particular bridges, unusual vehicles) and indeed to the downright random (e.g. dew drops on a spider's web, or a Japanese 'lucky cat' charm – two genuine examples from recent UK exams).

The following is a possible characterisation of what expert physicists are able to do which allows them to succeed when presented with such questions.

1. Expert physicists are able to identify the *essential* physical features of the given situation, as well as what might be non-essential and fruitful to ignore, simplify or approximate.

2. Expert physicists can then *codify* the essential features of the situation to produce an accurate 'physics representation' or 'physics model' of that situation – this will usually have diagrammatic, mathematical and/or graphical components.

3. Expert physicists can then work logically, and usually mathematically, with these representations to gain insight (solve the problem set).

Reading Collins et al.'s paper 'Cognitive Apprenticeship' led me to consider the visibility of the cognitive processes that occur at each step.

I think the cognitive processes involved in step 3 are usually more visible to students. Step 3 is essentially 'showing your working', which is frequently modelled and demanded by physics teachers. It also tends to be somewhat procedural once the correct equations or diagrams (physics representations) are set up.

Therefore, I think it is the 'setting up' processes of steps 1 and 2 that are usually much less visible to students. When students struggle with higher-level physics, they often say, 'I understand the ideas in class and all the maths when we go through questions, but I just can't do questions myself. I can't work out how to get started on them.' This would seem to support my suggestion that it is the *initial* cognitive processes involved with solving physics problems (steps 1 and 2) that are the least visible. Steps 1 and 2 might occur fairly instantly and automatically in a physics teacher's mind upon being presented with a question, and so they might proceed to codification (producing the physics model) without really making explicit exactly *how* they produced that particular representation. What features of the question did they particularly notice? What were they thinking as they were reading? At what points did they pause, go back and re-read, or switch focus from text to diagram and back to text again? Which specific feature of the question prompted the realisation about which physical principles or laws they needed to use?

Remembering to give this kind of detailed metacognitive commentary about *how you got to* the correct working, *before* starting to present it, can really help students learn *what they should be thinking (and doing)* when they are trying to get started on a physics problem. This could occur during teacher-led review of homework or assessment questions, but also during instruction, where the teacher-led metacognitive commentary could be gradually reduced as the class works through a sequence of questions.

The following activity also works quite well to make the expert cognitive processes in steps 1 and 2 more visible. It would probably be best to teacher-model this activity first so students get the most out of it. Students are given a problem-solving exam question with a full-marks answer already written in. Ensure the students know that the answer given is fully correct, then ask students to answer a set of questions about the question, such as those below.

Analysis of a physics exam question

1. What physics is this question about (broad topic)? How can you tell this from the question?

2. What specific things do students need to *know* to answer this question?

3. What did students have to do (or realise) to answer this question?

4. What 'clues' were there in the question about how to do it? These could be obvious or more subtle.

5. Where was the key information in the question?

6. What information was actually irrelevant to answering the question?

7. If a student was stuck on this question, which part(s) of the question would you tell them to look at again, or what would you tell them to try doing, to help get them started on the right track?

The questions encourage students to look more closely at the question and the cognitive processes that were required to successfully answer it. Having the full-marks answer to refer to means students can focus fully on trying to understand *how* the question was successfully answered rather than worrying about trying to answer the question themselves.

Here are some further strategies which could help students pick up the expert thinking processes underpinning steps 1 and 2 of physics problem-solving:

- Teach physics knowledge explicitly and secure it; students won't be able to recognise the *essential* physical features of a situation if they don't *know* enough physics in the first place. Embed spaced retrieval practice into your routine teaching, and explicitly teach and provide resources for self-testing.

- Take opportunities to teach students some physics *disciplinary knowledge* – specifically, that in physics you are not only allowed to but supposed to make simplifications and approximations that sometimes seem laughable (such as the infamous physicist's spherical chicken). Make sure that common physics simplifications are taught explicitly – give students a list at the start of the course: no friction or air resistance; massless strings; rigid beams; no wind or interference; isolated systems. Objects are approximated as perfect geometric shapes, or reduced to 'point particles' with no height, width or depth and all their mass concentrated at a single point – so much easier to work with, mathematically, to gain insight. Setting order-of-magnitude, back-of-the-envelope estimation questions (Fermi questions), which cannot be solved without significant approximation, can really help with this.

- Make it clear that students need to not take contexts at face value, in all their rich and particular complexity, but rather should be asking themselves, 'What have I *basically* got here?' (in quite general terms, e.g. shape or component parts) and then, 'What physics concept springs to mind?' Examples include: a see-saw (moments), a spring (Hooke's law), an object moving through a fluid (terminal velocity), electricity in a magnetic field (the motor effect), electricity being generated (the generator effect), two resistors in series (a potential divider).

- Specifically teach students about the use of diagrams in physics and give them practice. This is no different to getting year 7s to practise 2D diagrams of lab equipment. A hot air balloon is a sphere (ignore the basket); a flute is just a tube of air which is open at both ends (ignore the keys). *Especially* make time to practise 'standard physics diagrams' like free-body diagrams, horizontal and vertical components of the initial velocity of a projectile, resolving weight forces for an object on a slope.

- Explicitly teach students how reading physics exam questions is different to reading other texts, e.g. a novel. Novels tend to be read linearly, whereas when I read a complex physics problem this is very nonlinear: diagrams are scanned and constantly checked against the text, annotations occur all the time – on the answer line, in the margins, on or alongside the diagrams. Try narrating, or even mapping, your reading process to a class as you tackle a problem, to demonstrate to students just how *active* this process is.

- Explicitly tell students that not every detail in a physics exam question will be important. Look carefully at that diagram of an electric toothbrush, and you'll see the question is *really* about electrical transformers. Point out when the context of a question turns out to be entirely irrelevant: a question which asked 'Explain how infrasound travels through the Earth's crust' actually required no knowledge of infrasound or the Earth's crust, only that infrasound was a longitudinal wave (which the question told you) – and all longitudinal waves travel the same way, so you 'just reel off' that standard explanation.

- Explicitly draw students' attention to what they should be thinking when they see certain things. 'As soon as you see a potential divider circuit, you should be thinking RATIOS! As soon as you see a thermistor, draw the graph (of resistance against temperature) – which you can then work with and annotate, freeing up your working memory.'

- Insist that students highlight or circle all numerical data given in a question, and make a 'shopping list' of what they know using algebraic symbols. This should jog their memory of a relevant equation which may be of use.

- Use a 'manifestations grid' knowledge organiser as a five-minute activity at the end of the topic (one minute to fill in, four minutes to share ideas) to ensure students are aware that a single physics idea, law or principle has very many possible manifestations, all of which could be set as contexts for examination questions.

All of these pedagogic techniques tease out the thinking required by expert physicists to codify the essential features of a situation to produce an accurate representation/model of that situation. They all, in one way or another, exemplify the principles articulated in Collins et al.'s 'Cognitive Apprenticeship' paper, and help apprentice physicists grow their expertise.

SCIENCE

BY BETH HARTWELL

As scientists, we usually take our interdisciplinary knowledge for granted. We can easily make links across each discipline, and understand how physics, biology and chemistry rely on each other. Using and linking knowledge across disciplines is a key element when thinking scientifically. It allows us to formulate rational conclusions based on all scientific knowledge. In reality, scientists draw upon knowledge from all fields within their workplace. Their teams are usually composed of colleagues with a mixture of disciplines working towards a common goal. Experts combine knowledge from each subject to strengthen their hypotheses, accumulate their evidence base, and, finally, articulate their theories.

We must ensure that the links between the disciplines are explicitly taught to ensure that our students have a holistic approach to their practice. Emphasising the links ensures that key threshold concepts are addressed thoroughly. This allows for preconceptions and misconceptions to be addressed, which is critical as we know that many threshold concepts impact future understanding (Holman and Yeomans, 2018). A basic example at key stage 3 is understanding simple chemical reactions and then applying this knowledge whilst teaching the reaction of respiration. Explicitly teaching respiration this way ensures that strategic knowledge surrounding chemical reactions is embedded, with it also minimising misconceptions which might arise when teaching respiration (especially the confusion that many students face when they believe respiration is breathing).

Before we teach the thinking process behind making cross-disciplinary linkages through explicit instruction, it is critical to ensure that the sequence of our curriculum builds upon threshold concepts which span the science curriculum, rather than planning individual subjects in their own entity. At key stage 3, it may sound obvious to teach chemical reactions before respiration or particles before sound. As we get more specialised going through into key stage 4 and 5, I would argue that cross-subject sequencing conversations are critical, ensuring that scientific knowledge is built upon as a whole rather than each individual subject planning their own sequence. Throughout the curriculum design process, highlighting the linkages is important to ensure that our interdisciplinary approach isn't lost within the classroom.

Articulating the links within the curriculum is the most important tool to ensure that students are forming these connections. It's a case of making the connections clear and visible. This simply starts with explicit instruction which explains our expert thinking. For example, when teaching radioactivity in the classroom, explicitly refer to links within both the chemistry content (atomic structure and the periodic table) and biology knowledge (ionisation of DNA molecules within the nucleus of cells causing mutation or uncontrolled growth by cell division). It is rare that students have 'the externalization of processes that are usually carried out internally' which is critical when linking the curriculum together.

Here is a list of connections which you can use with students to exemplify the links across the science curriculum:

Biology

- When teaching photosynthesis and respiration ⟹ chemical reactions (chemistry), changes in energy (physics)

- When teaching enzymes ⟹ rates of reaction (chemistry), kinetic energy (physics)

- When teaching diffusion, osmosis, active transport ⟹ particle arrangement (chemistry), rates of reaction (chemistry), kinetic energy (physics)

Chemistry

- When teaching chemistry of the atmosphere ⟹ photosynthesis and respiration (biology), non-renewable resources (physics)

- When teaching properties and structures ⟹ electrical conductivity (physics)

- When teaching atomic structure ⟹ atomic structure (physics), biological molecules (biology)

Physics

- When teaching radioactivity ⟹ atomic structure and the periodic table (chemistry), ionisation of DNA molecules within the nucleus of cells causing mutation or uncontrolled growth by cell division (biology)

- When teaching electricity $\Rightarrow$ atomic structure and metallic bonding (chemistry), nerve cells/the nervous system/electric impulses (biology)

- When teaching energy $\Rightarrow$ photosynthesis and respiration (biology), endothermic and exothermic reactions (chemistry)

- When teaching light and sound $\Rightarrow$ the eye and the ear (biology)

As our students develop confidence, we can then scaffold classroom discussions based on existing prior knowledge. For example, when looking at learning how light travels through the eye within biology, it is critical that we revisit learning carried out in physics: 'Why is your physics knowledge on light so important here?' Explicitly creating these links is important. It increases conceptual knowledge, and ultimately increases understanding of knowledge within both the physics curriculum and the biology curriculum. It minimises the chance of students learning isolated scientific facts without a grasp of the core concept or understanding.

Over time, depending on the students in front of you, you could fade the teacher scaffold. This increases independence and aids self-regulation. Asking students to recall everything they know about the structure of an atom (within their chemistry lessons) before teaching radiation in physics directly links the two concepts together. This could also be supported with diagrams, discussions and modelling. They must articulate their knowledge clearly before more difficult concepts are taught. The critical aspect is that students will need to recall, monitor and reflect on their prior learning, allowing them to view the new learning that is about to take place through the lens of their current understanding of their related scientific knowledge.

After learning has taken place, the exploration of the links also strengthens conceptual knowledge and helps students apply factual knowledge. A simple mind mapping strategy can enable students to summarise their new learning – including links to different parts of the science curriculum, e.g. refraction when discussing the eye – and form schemas which they can draw upon when building on this knowledge in further study. Independent exploration must come with a caveat: recalling and linking interdisciplinary knowledge is difficult. We must ensure that the expert thinking process has been explicitly shown to the students via teacher modelling throughout the teaching process before we allow them to explore linkages independently.

Allocating time in the curriculum to revisit, embed and reflect on these critical concepts allows students to build conceptual knowledge and confidence within core fundamental concepts. Starting with explicit instruction and fading teacher scaffolding over time, increasing student independence when exploring and identifying linkages will develop a learner who has more secure knowledge.

We must ensure that articulating expert thinking has a place within our curriculum, and time must be spent to address this. We must not feel we need to rush through the curriculum with such pace that critical reviews and reflections are missed. Ultimately, taking the time to embed knowledge and understanding throughout the curriculum ensures that threshold concepts are secure in the students' minds, and developing this expert thinking process will enable students to thrive throughout their 'scientific' career.

METHOD
Ways to promote the development of expertise

For 'method' read 'methods of teaching'. Here Collins et al. outline six elements of apprenticeship-style teaching, beginning with the teacher *modelling* a task or process and the students observing. *Scaffolding* support helps the students complete a task. Next, the teacher observes the student whilst *coaching* them to complete the task. The next stage of the teaching methods process is for students to *articulate* what they know and how they think when they complete the task. When the task is complete, teachers show students how to *reflect* upon their performance and compare it with the performance of others. The final method stage is to ask students to identify and then solve their own problems; the level of teacher guidance is faded and the tasks allow greater student *exploration*.

METHOD
Ways to promote the development of expertise

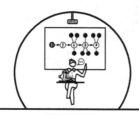

MODELLING
Teacher performs a task so students
can observe

COACHING
Teacher observes and facilitates
while students perform a task

SCAFFOLDING
Teacher provides supports to help the
student perform a task

ARTICULATION
Teacher encourages students to
verbalize their knowledge and thinking

REFLECTION
Teacher enables students to compare
their performance with others

EXPLORATION
Teacher invites students to pose and
solve their own problems

A summary introduction to Dimension Two:
METHOD

According to Tom Lund, 'computational thinking' appears to many students to be common sense, which means that the processes inherent in computational thinking need 'to be made visible, in order to counter many students' propensity to dive headfirst into programming tasks and consequently make simple and avoidable mistakes'. Tom provides a transparent guide to modelling-based methods that help students learn the fundamental thinking behind computer science.

Design can be a challenge. Stephen Foreman explains succinctly how to go beyond the blank page, using Collins et al.'s methods for making thinking visible. As Stephen comments, 'unlocking the thinking process behind constructing abstract designs ... is key to subject understanding and, ultimately, to becoming an expert designer'.

A literary critic has a very clear analytical thought process, one that teachers share. But, as Donal Hale explains, 'this disciplinary thinking has become second nature; however, for apprentices of English, this will not be the case'. Donal's detailed description of how he develops students' thought processes in an incredibly thorough way to write fluently about *An Inspector Calls* is exemplary. And Huntington's deputy headteacher and SENDCO, Gail Naish, shows beautifully how 'the power of image is a key to cut through [learning] barrier[s] and engage and build memory' for those students with special educational needs.

Catherine Campbell and Jane Elsworth explain how they engage their students' thinking methodically, so that they look at any issue facing them 'through the cognitive lens of a geographer'. The thinking processes their students develop enable them 'to show a real depth of understanding, make evidence-informed judgements and draw valid conclusions'.

Who knew that a fundamental thinking process for unpicking a text in German requires an approach 'much more aligned to mathematical problem-solving rather than, ironically, the reading model outlined in Collins et al.'s "cognitive apprenticeship" paper'? Well, read Cherry Bailey's enlightening chapter and all will become clear.

This section finishes with Julie Kettlewell. Her chapter provides us with a detailed account of how far Collins et al.'s thinking has been developed. She teaches her psychology students to think expertly by following 'the seven-step model outlined in the EEF's *Metacognition and Self-Regulated Learning* guidance report'. It is cognitive apprenticeship for the 2020s. The link between Collins et al.'s 'Cognitive Apprenticeship' paper, published 30 years ago, and the seven-step model, which is only three years old, is clear and illustrates just how educational researchers continually refine and build upon the work of their predecessors.

COMPUTER SCIENCE

All computer science qualifications challenge students to think like a subject expert. To be able to think like a computer scientist, a student must be able to 'think computationally'. This is the fundamental principle that is woven through all computer science qualifications, in line with the UK national curriculum (Department for Education, 2013).

Computational thinking includes two key elements: abstract thinking and decomposition. Computational thinking is mainly used during the practical programming units of the GCSE and A level qualifications, but it is also a feature of the theory examination. If students can develop their computational thinking, they can apply this disciplinary approach and can create concise, efficient, and robust solutions to many different programming problems.

How to teach the thinking process

To explain the teaching process of instilling computational thinking methods in a student's brain, it is best to use an example programming problem (OCR, 2020):

> Create a program that takes a time for a car going past a speed camera, the time going past the next one and the distance between them to calculate the average speed for the car in mph. The cameras are one mile apart. The registration of the car and its speed should be stored in an external text file as well as displayed on the screen.

This problem involves a simple program about speed cameras. Even though the problem is simple, the quality of student response can vary depending upon the level of computational thinking that has been used.

Abstract thinking

Abstract thinking is the process of removing any unnecessary details from the problem so that a programmer can make a concise program that only deals with the problem components that are solvable by a computer.

Using the example above, I would ask students to create two lists: *important characteristics* and *irrelevant characteristics*. This allows students to really think about the problem before even trying to create a coded solution. The most common mistake students make when programming is making a long-winded solution that does not fully solve the problem. Table 1 shows the abstraction of the problem.

Important Characteristics	Irrelevant Characteristics
The distance between the speed cameras	The type of vehicle
The speed limit on the road	Whether the cameras are forward or backward facing
The current time	How many people are in the vehicle
Vehicle registration	

Table 1 – Abstraction of speed camera problem

Following this abstraction, students should be able to note that the important characteristics of the problem are distance and time, both of which are required for calculating the speed of the vehicle. These details can then be taken to the next stage, decomposition.

Decomposition

Decomposition is the process of breaking the problem down into smaller more manageable chunks, precisely as recommended by Collins et al. when they write about 'executing the parts' of a problem, rather than tackling the whole challenge. Once this process is completed, students can create a structured program and reusable programming components, *subroutines*, to be used in their code or other programs in the future.

To teach this way of thinking to students, we go through the process of creating a top-down structure. Table 2 shows a simple decomposition of the speed camera problem.

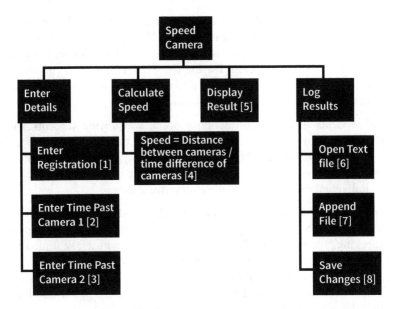

Table 2 – Top-down hierarchy chart

The numbered blocks show what the programmer needs to program. Not all blocks are numbered because the blocks that are underneath solve the block above. For example, by entering the registration and the time, all the requisite details have been successfully entered. The problem should be tackled from left to right to complete the full answer.

The mode of thinking from the previous section needs to be made visible, in order to counter many students' propensity to dive headfirst into programming tasks and consequently make simple and avoidable mistakes. As Collins et al. point out, the way that this thinking is brought to the surface is by using elements of the cognitive apprenticeship process:

- Modelling
- Coaching
- Scaffolding
- Articulation
- Reflection
- Exploration

During my teaching practice, I use **modelling** on the board and flipchart paper with groups so that they can all see my thinking process when I tackle problems. The process of thinking is also narrated so that students can see how the process evolves in my brain. During the narration, targeted questioning, using Bloom's taxonomy (EEF, 2018), is also used so that students have a chance to assist and contribute to the solution of the task.

To aid students with the abstraction process, we provide students with a **scaffolded** table which is partially completed. As they practise, the scaffold is faded, until they have a blank table. This is repeated as we teach them decomposition. **Coaching** would then be used to help support students learning on an individual basis in a mixed prior attainment group.

The next stage of the teaching process is to allow students to **explore** different ways to complete a computing problem from start to finish while implementing the thinking process. The students would be provided with a task similar to the example above. Students would then try to create a programmed solution using the thinking processes from computational thinking. Students can struggle with this, but it is important for them to experience challenge and to become comfortable with feeling uncomfortable.

Once students have attempted a problem independently, they then go on to reflect upon the process. **Reflection** is extremely important when it comes to student learning. As Collins et al. note, 'reflection should allow students to compare their work to the expert and other students'. To aid with the reflection process, students work in well-regulated groups, where each one has a defined length of time to reflect upon their attempt and to critique each other's work.

It is, perhaps, easy to view computational thinking as basic common sense. But if students are not trained how to think abstractly and how to undertake the decomposition of the task, they soon get lost when trying to create a computer program. Here a student was tasked with creating a music player which can create and provide playlists:

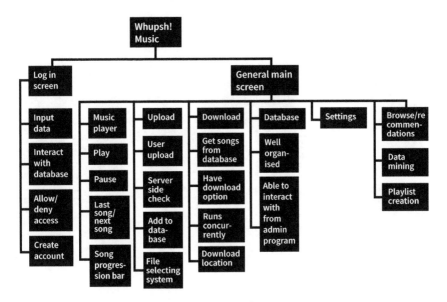

Figure 1 – Decomposition of music player task

If he had not been well trained through the cognitive apprenticeship process to think computationally, he could not have produced such a complex program. As Collins et al. make clear, we need to sequence 'meaningful tasks [which] gradually increase in difficulty'. Compared to the simple decomposition of the speed camera problem in table 2 above, figure 1 illustrates how the student has taken his thinking to a deeper level whilst abiding by the fundamental computational thinking processes.

DESIGN TECHNOLOGY

BY STEPHEN FOREMAN

Teaching design operates at two levels: firstly, cultivating in students the cognitive skills to develop an idea to the point of the production process; secondly, the teaching of practical skills which enable the competent production of an artefact. For the design technology teacher, Collins et al.'s 'Cognitive Apprenticeship' paper delineates several teaching techniques which operate at both levels. In this essay, I will focus upon how to develop students' initial thinking when faced with a design brief.

Expert designers visualise initial ideas, then understand how to think through the intricacies of progressing a design before modelling physical outcomes. Expert designers demonstrate a heightened sense of visual awareness. They can articulate ideas through drawing using a range of different techniques they have learned, developed and honed over time. Expert designers then use practical skills to test out theories about how materials perform during technological processes. Finally, expert designers bring all those strands together and produce an artefact which meets the design brief.

The fundamentals of cognitive apprenticeship enable students to develop the largely amorphous creative skills which are the heart of great design work.

Students assume that successful designers are grown rather than taught. Such notions can negatively impact upon students' confidence; they quickly become scared of failure.

If we try to deconstruct the thinking process of an expert designer, we find, initially, that it is not a consciously thought-through process. Over time, it will have become what one might call, dangerously perhaps, a 'natural' process; I say 'dangerously' because for students it can seem like an innate/'natural' skill that they either possess or they don't. Our role is to surface the seemingly 'natural'.

Unlocking the thinking process behind constructing abstract designs and creative concepts is key to subject understanding and, ultimately, to becoming an expert designer. Identifying these skills can sometimes be difficult to articulate in the classroom. The job of the teacher is to distil this process and make it become real for students. We can teach the process through cognitive apprenticeship and students can first visualise and then, ultimately, learn it through repeated practice.

Whether we can think without language is a debate for another time and place, but the design brief is where we begin, and the design brief is expressed in words. Collins et al. explain clearly the modelling, scaffolding, fading and coaching process which is central to teaching the expert thinking processes of the designer. The words of the brief are where we begin.

When developing the students' cognitive processes so that they think like designers, I begin by taking the key content words of the brief and, using old-school flipcharts or a whiteboard, I model how I would express my initial response to a brief. It is important to practise. All teachers perform in the classroom, but modelling the thinking processes of the expert designer requires pre-performance rehearsal. Consequently, I practise hard beforehand, and know not just what ideas I will come up with, but also what I will express about my thinking, metacognitively, as I arrive at those ideas.

The flipcharts are copied by students onto A3 blank paper folded into quarters, the sections used to delineate the different elements of the responses and to segment thinking. It is important to get them to write down and sketch what I produce *verbatim*, as it is their record of my expert design thought process.

In this first stage of teaching how to think like a designer, there are parallels with writing poetry. In his book *Poetry in the Making*, Ted Hughes comments that, 'In our brains there are many mansions, and most of the doors are locked, and the keys inside.' Once I have modelled my own expert design thinking processes for students, one of the things that I find helps unlock those Hughesian doors in our students' brains is an energy-filled – and energy-sapping for all involved – lesson where students have one design brief and four lots of eight minutes to write down their own ideas in response to the brief.

At the beginning of the second lesson, students are given another piece of A3 paper, which is again quartered, and a pencil. The dividing of the paper, by simple folding, is a subtle way of reducing the fear of the blank page. Complete silence, bar the teacher's cajoling. The lesson requires the teacher to prowl the room, poking and prodding students' imaginations, counting down the time, creating a sense of urgency. You cannot give the students time to come up for air. If anyone thinks s/he has come to an end, insist upon one more idea. No stopping. Fill the page. The concentrated experience is exhausting for everyone.

This second lesson has two key objectives. The first is for the students to mimic the expert design thinking process you have modelled in the first lesson. The second is to drive out the incapacitating fear of the blank page. There is *always* one more idea.

The lesson finishes with a metacognitive debrief. Explore with the students what they felt about the process, what they found helpful, what surprised them, what they found challenging.

The third lesson returns to teacher modelling. This time, I take my flipchart response to a brief from lesson one and make explicit my thinking processes as I decide which of my ideas I want to develop further. Again, this lesson requires significant rehearsal of metacognitive thinking. The students write down, verbatim, what I am thinking as well as my design sketches and commentary, all of which I articulate on a new sheet of flipchart paper.

One of the things I emphasise is the frequent back-and-forth between my developing ideas and the brief. That connection is a fundamental aspect of good design: when they come to the final stage of the design process – evaluating the finished artefact against the initial design brief – they are so much better prepared if you can get them to connect their thinking with the brief throughout the development process.

The students then, in silence, mimic my thinking during this next stage of the design process with one of their four designs from the second lesson. The to-and-fro between modelling and scaffolding is crucial to developing the students' thinking.

In the fourth lesson, I like to identify three examples which exemplify the best work from students across the full range of prior attainment. I talk through the ideas aloud, asking the student to explain certain aspects of their developmental thinking and decision making. I emphasise the rigour of the process and keep bringing the discussion back to the relationship between the ideas and the brief.

To extend the link between writing poetry and expert design thinking, the pressures upon the poet and the designer imposed by working within constraining frameworks – for the poet that might be the rhymes and rhythms of the sonnet form; for the budding classroom designer, that might be something as simple as the time constraints insisted upon by the teacher – are productive pressures which enable, rather than inhibit, the creative process.

In lesson five, the next stage of the design process is the physical modelling of the amorphous idea which exists just in the students' minds and on the A3 paper. Physically modelling the developing ideas allows the cognitive process to materialise from the A3 page by having ideas represented in tangible three-dimensional form.

The physicality of having a 'real' design or idea in front of a student can be very powerful in fostering design confidence. The process speaks to their inner child! At this relatively early stage of the process, students can simply create a *plasticine* form or a card model held together with masking tape, the idea being that these three dimensional forms are constructed relatively quickly. Conversely the model can be expressed by an extremely complex computer-aided design model of their developing design, although this will take much longer to construct – and arguably, either performs the same cognitive function. From this point on in the design process, the teacher direction fades and the coaching role, on an individual student basis, takes over.

One might argue that overcoming the imaginative hurdle presented by the blank page is a design student's biggest challenge. The structured process, delineated here over five lessons, replicates many features of Collins et al.'s 'Cognitive Apprenticeship', making the amorphous, opaque thought processes of the expert designer visible to all students.

ENGLISH

When teaching students how to write effective essays in English, especially ones that may be termed 'argumentative essays', we aim to instil in students what we would call a critical style. For teachers, experts in their discipline, this disciplinary thinking has become second nature; however, for apprentices of English, this will not be the case, and therefore requires teachers to teach in a manner where such complex thinking is visible to our students.

To illustrate how this cognitive process can be explicitly taught to students, this chapter will exemplify how the principles of cognitive apprenticeship apply to the teaching of an argumentative essay based on the GCSE text *An Inspector Calls*.

The four essential aspects of cognitive apprenticeship

To achieve the ultimate aim of using 'explicit modelling of expert processes', Collins et al. outline four essential ingredients required in any attempt to make thinking visible to learners:

1. Modelling

2. Scaffolding

3. Fading

4. Coaching

Modelling

Modelling in English will invariably involve unpicking a model essay response with students, led by the teacher. There will likely be discussion of its strengths and weaknesses, but this approach has inherent flaws. Put simply, students are unlikely 'to make use of potential models of good writing acquired through reading because they have no understanding of how authors produced such text'.

Live modelling provides a potential solution to this. Whilst some teachers may feel nervous at this prospect, it is the best 'model of instruction that works to make thinking visible'. This is the optimal approach to unearthing the complex thought processes that contribute to successful essay writing. It works by teachers scripting an essay out loud whilst providing a running commentary of their justifications for their writing choices.

For example, consider the script below of the teacher modelling how the apprentice might approach the reading and highlighting of key words in the Mrs Birling question:

EXAMPLE 1

Teacher: So with this question, there is an important 'hinge phrase' here that opens up the argument: 'How far...'. So, I am going to highlight this and underline it. Now, this is a typical phrase used by examiners, which is similar to 'To what extent do you agree?' This is important because the question goes on to say whether I think Mrs B is unlikeable, so underline and circle that phrase, and how far she could be read that way. Most would agree she is unlikeable, but this question type hints that you might want to consider an alternative reading too. Can anyone think of a reason why Mrs B is perhaps a sympathetic character?

Students' instincts may lead them to focus too heavily on the phrase 'an unlikeable character', merely writing an essay that exemplifies a singular interpretation of the character's unlikeability. This limits students' thinking. Notice how the teacher adopts the term 'hinge phrase' as a method of thinking that shows an actual line of argument needs to be established. And even before we have got to this point, the teacher has defined and explained a 'hinge phrase', for a teacher can never assume student understanding. Getting to the nub of what students understand is a bit like peeling back the layers of an onion. With every layer of meaning explained, a new level of meaning is revealed which, incredibly, needs explaining. Effective checking of understanding is often a revelatory experience.

Finally, the teacher invokes a debate by considering a sympathetic view of the character to be interrogated.

Below are examples of students' approach to unpicking an exam question before (with a similar question style, but based on another character) and after this modelling process.

EXAMPLE 2

Before:

How far does Priestley present **Sheila** as the character **who changes most** in the play?

After:　　→ *to what extent do you agree?*

How far does Priestley present **Mrs Birling** as an **unlikeable** character?

↘ *sympathetic?*

The 'before' example is revealing. Was that student thinking there was even an argument to develop here? Would they have considered whether Sheila has not changed in some ways, as the teacher models in the second example?

Scaffolding

Scaffolding 'can range from doing almost the entire task for them to giving occasional hints as to what to do next'. Below is an example of how a teacher might use scaffolding to support the writing of a short introduction that establishes a line of argument that began through the modelling of unpicking the question itself. The teacher in this instance is live modelling an introduction, using a visualiser, whilst providing a commentary on their writing choices:

EXAMPLE 3

Writing	Commentary
Whilst Mrs Birling is **seemingly** an unlikeable character, Priestley presents her as more complex than that. Although she shows **contempt** towards the working classes and adopts a sense of **superiority** over others based on class, she is merely a **product** of the Edwardian class system.	I use whilst to begin to create a sense of debate the question implies [pause whilst writing (pww)] and the word **seemingly** to reinforce that [pww]. I then move to outline arguments on either side so [pww] I am going to mention her contempt for working classes and [writing] and something about her [pww] before I bring in this counter-point about her [pww] being a product of her society.

In the first instance, the teacher is modelling the entire task for them to make the thinking and writing processes visible to students. Notice how the student below is replicating the argumentative style of essay writing but using their own lexical choices:

EXAMPLE 4

~~Mrs Birling~~ Whilst Mrs Birling may be considered unlikeable, Priestley presents her in other ways too. She does show prejudice towards people who are working class, but maybe that is because she is influenced by the Edwardian class system.

Further use of scaffolding can then come in various other forms when students practise writing their own introductions, including, but not limited to:

- Using sentence stems (e.g. 'Whilst Mrs Birling is seemingly an unlikeable character...') and blanking out the core content of the arguments for students to write their own

- Providing students with a 'vocabulary box' to use within their own writing (e.g. 'whilst/although', 'seemingly/appears to be')

- Unpicking the grammatical constructions (e.g. 'Begin with a complex sentence that hints at two sides of argument')

Fading

There might be a worry at this stage that such a method relies too heavily on scaffolding and does not promote students' independence in essay writing. This is why 'fading' is crucial as this encompasses 'the notion of slowly removing the support, giving the apprentice more and more responsibility'.

You could do this in various different ways, but my suggestion would be to live model a main-body paragraph of the essay, which concerns much evaluative thinking and requires exemplification from the text, analysis of authorial methods and relevant contextual linking. The example below contains a paragraph, from the same teacher as above, that was live modelled, and then coded to meet the requirements common to mark schemes:

EXAMPLE 5

Priestley presents Mrs Birling as '*a rather cold woman*' and her husband's '*social superior*' in the **opening stage directions. The immediate impression, therefore, she will create for the audience is that of the icily, wealthier, privileged 'upper class'** <u>typical of the Edwardian era in some parts of society.</u> **Priestley, in essence, intends for the audience to hold a prejudice against her** of an uncaring woman right from the beginning, which is **reinforced by her opening lines** where she instructs Edna that '*I'll ring from the drawing room when we want coffee*'. The audience is given a full sense of her privileged status and is <u>made clear to viewers in post-war Britain that such figures are out of touch with the plight of the average person.</u>

Bold = role of the writer and authorial methods

Italics = range of textual evidence

<u>Underlined = relevant links to contextual factors</u>

Students then, independently, apply their learning of the teacher-as-expert's thinking processes by writing the next paragraph of the essay, highlighting where they met the criteria (in the early stages, before it becomes increasingly second nature to them) as illustrated below:

EXAMPLE 6

Later in the play, **Priestley shows other examples of her icy nature towards the lower classes,** especially Eva. When referring to Eva **she uses dismissive remarks** like *'girls of that class'* and *'as if a girl of that sort would refuse money'.* The use of the determiner 'that' shows her as a typical snob, **the type Priestley wants us to think she is.** She sees Eva as a subhuman and inferior to her. <u>This might be a comment on how many wealthier Edwardians truly felt about lower-class people.</u>

Bold = role of the writer and authorial methods

Italics = range of textual evidence

<u>Underlined = relevant links to contextual factors</u>

Coaching

The next step is not necessarily a continuation of the previous ones; rather, 'coaching is the thread running through the entire apprenticeship experience; [it] is the process of overseeing the student's learning'. Collins et al. offer an array of examples of how coaching occurs, which includes:

- Evaluating the activities of apprentices and diagnosing the kinds of problems they are having
- Challenging them and offering encouragement
- Giving feedback

Much of this can be seen in the worked example. The teacher clearly diagnosed an issue with developing a line of argument from students' previous attempts with writing about Sheila **(EXAMPLE 2).** There are countless opportunities within the lesson to challenge and encourage students through targeted questioning, as seen when the teacher introduced an alternative interpretation to Mrs Birling **(EXAMPLE 4).**

Feedback would occur not only within the lesson but also subsequently during teachers' marking. In this instance, the teacher later asked students to examine essays on Sheila alongside essays on Mrs Birling and to conduct a comparative evaluation, thereby reinforcing the new cognitive processes modelled to them by their teacher.

DEVELOPING SEND STUDENTS' ANALYTICAL WRITING SKILLS

BY GAIL NAISH

Students with special educational needs and disabilities span the whole spectrum of attainment, but for the purposes of this piece, I have chosen to focus on supporting those young people with global learning needs (or moderate learning difficulties) who form the large proportion of children on the SEND register in our schools. Many of these young people will function at a reading age significantly below age expected levels.

Students with global learning needs find all aspects of reading and writing more of a challenge than their peers. They not only have significant challenges with receptive language and processing of knowledge and skills but also often struggle with memory retention and the pace of learning. These issues in secondary-age students have the potential to lead to low self-esteem and consequent frustration and disengagement with school if these needs go unaddressed.

In my experience, 'making learning and thinking visible' is truly essential in any classroom in which one is teaching students with global learning needs if those young people are to make progress and engage more fully with the school curriculum. An additional advantage, although by no means the most important, is that this approach empowers SEND students to be more effective in our current examination system, which is predicated on memory retention and recall as a means of achieving 'success'.

I have chosen to write about the importance of using visual images in the teaching of reading for students with SEND. Since text and the written word are a challenge for students with a reading age significantly below their chronological one, the power of image is a key to cut through this barrier and engage and build memory. My focus in this piece will be on how a disciplined approach should draw on the connection of images and text to truly 'make thinking visible'. As Collins et al. have suggested, it is essential 'to situate the abstract tasks of the school curriculum to contexts that make sense to students'.

An expert teacher of reading will go beyond the mere phonic sounding-out of text, to a deeper understanding of inference and context. They will encourage their students to question a text, asking why the writer has chosen those particular words.

The toolkit which I developed alongside my former colleague Abigail Brierley allowed us to make those abstract concepts tangible and concrete for our SEND students. We summarised the eight key reading skills required to be proficient in both decoding and inferring meaning. We attached a specific image to each concept. These images were then systematically revisited throughout all our teaching materials and classroom display. This allowed students to have a 'shorthand for text'.

These skills and related images are shown below:

- Information retrieval
- Inference
- Empathy (standing in other people's shoes)
- Asking questions
- Making judgements
- Making predictions
- Identifying the 'hooks' which the writer is using
- Making connections with other texts

The concrete images became the shorthand for representing and reinforcing the name of the reading skills being taught: for example, the retriever dog for 'picking out information from a text'; the crystal ball for 'predicting what might happen next'; someone else's shoes for 'demonstrating empathy'; etc.

The cognitive apprentice student reader began to learn from the expert teacher how to summarise text in their own words and form a more sophisticated response to the text. This probing approach allows the apprentice reader to recognise other viewpoints and feelings which may challenge or contradict their own. They can stand back from a text and question it.

As the pictures were used throughout every lesson, the routine and repetition **scaffolded** the students' memory retention and ability to recall. As these images were used consistently as a model of how to approach and engage with texts, over time the apprentice students began to embed the reading skills in their long-term memory. This 'dual coding' approach is so incredibly effective in supporting students' comprehension, it has now become a practised daily habit for my pedagogical planning. It has had tangible effects on students' progress as well as their confidence and sense of autonomy in the classroom.

This richly visual pedagogical approach can be demonstrated in the slide below from a scheme of learning for teaching Shakespeare's *Macbeth* to the KS3 nurture class, which includes a significant number of young people with SEND.

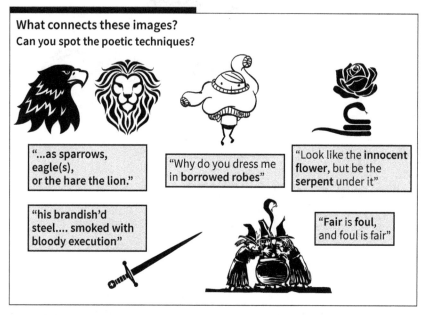

This slide simply demonstrates the connection of tangible images to the language of the play. As these combinations of images and written words were repeatedly revisited, students' memory retention was enhanced to the point that Shakespeare quotations could be recalled in the absence of the text being there.

This approach, however, goes beyond mere 'rote learning' and Pavlovian iteration of quotation on demand. Rich, nurturing and probing classroom talk is essential when exploring the metaphorical and implied meanings in the writer's language. An expert English teacher uses talk as a tool to allow their students to hear and then use sophisticated vocabulary and structures, making meaning from abstract ideas. The **modelling** of this thinking shifts over time from formulaic steps to fluid and more instinctive second nature. Collins et al. refer to the movement from **modelling** and **scaffolding** to **fading**, allowing for greater levels of student independence.

In my experience, this simple approach of using images to demystify abstract thinking can be applied to any scheme of learning or task. It has the power to be cross-curricular in its approach and application. It has demonstrated to me the ability to empower vulnerable and SEND learners to engage with the richness of literature and language, rather than just offering them simplified or modified versions. The apprentices truly develop their own mastery, as well as improving their own sense of self-worth, enjoyment and engagement in reading.

GEOGRAPHY

BY CATHERINE CAMPBELL & JANE ELSWORTH

One of the most challenging issues for students of geography to overcome is the fact that their experience of the world is often limited, and their daily lives can significantly differ from those of people in other places. Therefore, their awareness of and capacity to understand unfamiliar issues and places can be hampered.

As children and young people, many will have a lived experience of only one place, although they may have visited other places to see family or to go on holiday. Very few would have seen, first hand, how people's everyday lives across the world may have simple joys and opportunities as well as varied challenges. Furthermore, developing their understanding of how places came to be as they are, how the role of their heritage and the natural environment have changed over time, provides further challenges for young people to comprehend otherness, as they are likely to have experienced very little change over time themselves.

Ultimately, building in their minds a **sense of place** and supporting students to **think 'like a geographer'** are the key thought processes that will help them to become expert geographers. Developing their thinking processes can be done in the classroom through the principles of cognitive apprenticeship and then applied through regular opportunities for fieldwork.

Sense of place

In order to develop students' empathy and understanding of the lives of others – and how this may change over time – we must develop their thinking about a **sense of place**. Place itself has numerous definitions, from the simple – 'a space or location with meaning' – to more complex – 'an area having unique physical and human characteristics interconnected with other places' (www.nationalgeographic.org). But a sense of place is more than this. It is the ability to understand the context within which an issue or event occurs – for example, the level of development, the physical factors, any socioeconomic issues and, increasingly, political decision-making. As with all disciplinary thinking, students cannot think in a disciplinary way if they do not know and understand the content about which they are attempting to think.

Thinking 'like a geographer'

When approaching the study of geography, students need to develop their ability to identify and question the issues presented in a place. As students become more expert, they acquire a range of skills and methods to facilitate their thinking. One example from a recent fieldwork trip that illustrates the need for this explicit teaching about how to think like a geographer, even within a place that students have some knowledge of, is outlined below.

To support the study of river features and management at KS3, we take all our year 8 students out for the morning to walk along the River Ouse in York (a short coach ride from our school which is a few miles to the north of York city centre).

The students are usually a little disappointed to hear that they are 'only going into York' for this trip and many express some familiarity with the well-used riverside path we walk along in the pre-trip lessons. However, when we are on our trip, numerous students show that they have never *thought* about the river and its surroundings as a geographer before. They claim to have never even noticed any of the different flood defence systems in place or, if they have, they have failed to identify them as being for that purpose. They have never been prompted to *think* about local businesses or residents or hear about their experience of living and working by a river that regularly bursts its banks.

When we ask them to look at the place through the eyes of a geographer, they do so by working through the tasks in their field notebook, which prompt, structure and broaden their thinking and help explain what they can see and how it works. The students can see us modelling the thinking process and can start to practise these skills for themselves. The geographical concepts that support this thinking are often categorised in the following ways:

- Type of issue and context – physical or human, level of development of the place

- Scale of the issue – local, regional, national, global

- Processes involved – cause, effect, management and responses

- Impacts – primary or secondary, socioeconomic, environmental, cultural and political

- Change over time – long or short term

- Asking great questions – 5 Ws (who, where, what, when, why), how, the inquiry process

- Analysis – to compare and contrast, look for patterns and anomalies, assess sustainability

The prompt list is one of Collins et al.'s heuristics for problem-solving: it 'focuses student observation on the use and management of specific heuristics' to complete the field work systematically.

With practice in the classroom, through presenting representations of different places across the globe, in different contexts, we train our students to work through the thinking processes required to analyse, as objectively as they can, each unique place until the thought processes are hardwired into their brains. It is this hardwiring that is the key to developing a thinking geographer, and making that thinking explicit through modelling, scaffolding and fading the use of disciplinary thinking checklists is key to the hardwiring process.

An example of how we might support and develop both a sense of place and geographical thinking – comparing earthquakes in countries of contrasting levels of development

Our example we use is the 2010 earthquake in Port-au-Prince, Haiti alongside the 2011 earthquake in Christchurch, New Zealand.

To introduce this task, we make students aware of the places to be studied and the context of each location, including aspects such as the climate, natural landscape, levels of development and quality of life. To do this, we **model** the analysis of certain development indicators (figure 1) to allow the students to see the context and to begin to make comparisons. We also provide students with the data for the UK to allow them to relate the information provided to a place with which they are familiar. This is accompanied by maps and images (figure 1) of each place, which can be powerful tools in encouraging students to visualise and begin to develop their sense of place. These images show the clear contrast between the two countries and their levels of development.

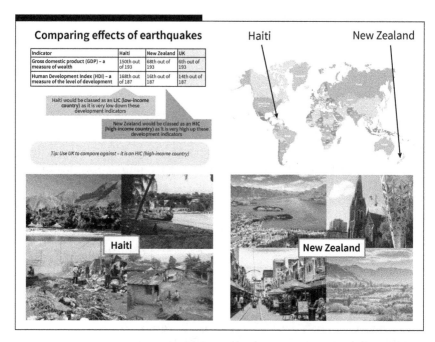

Figure 1: Providing context for each example

The second stage of the process requires students to investigate the earthquakes themselves with us **scaffolding** the process through asking them questions which guide them to each earthquake's characteristics, such as the strength, depth and location relative to the tectonics and the settlements they affected. This is vital before looking at the impacts of each example and beginning to question how and why there were significant differences in the scale and type of effects each place suffered.

At stage 3, students are then provided with information about the impacts of each earthquake (figure 2):

Christchurch, New Zealand

185 deaths, over half in the Canterbury TV building.	Estimated cost was $40 Billion dollars.
3129 injured.	100,000 buildings damaged, 10,000 of which had to be demolished. This was not helped by a previous earthquake in 2010 which weakened the buildings.
Christchurch cathedral lost its spire.	In a survey, 33% of all people who answered, stated they had suffered financial problems because of the earthquake.
Christchurch was no longer able to host any games during the 2011 rugby world cup.	Schools had to merge together.

Port-au-Prince, Haiti

Estimated 250,000 homes were destroyed.	316,000 people killed.
1 in 3 buildings in Port-au-Prince collapsed.	5,000 schools damaged or destroyed.
Total cost of repairs was approximately $11.5 Billion.	1.5 million were made homeless and put into 1,100 inadequate temporary camps.
Cholera claimed 4,350 lives in the aftermath of the earthquake, due to the temporary camps having poor and limited sanitation and clean water.	Hospitals and morgues that survived the quake, became overrun with dead.
The port, the airport and many roads around Port-au-Prince were completely destroyed (Primary effect).	

Figure 2: Impact statements for each example

The next step supports them to process the information as we **fade** our input. We show students how to code their information using categories, for example using codes for primary and secondary or social, economic and environmental impacts, and then leave them to complete their analysis.

From here, students begin to see patterns in the severity of impacts between their two contrasting case studies: greater loss of life, more damage to property and infrastructure in the low-income country of Haiti in comparison with the higher income country of New Zealand, where the cost of damage was higher.

The key here is for students to develop their ability to question why this has occurred and use what they understand about each place to explain it, having seen the process modelled, scaffolded and faded.

Students are required to link the sense of place they have developed, through the development indicators and context of the country, with the knowledge they have as expert geographers to **think through** the process required to analyse this information. Combining their sense of place with looking at the issue through the cognitive lens of a geographer enables students to show a real depth of understanding, make evidence-informed judgements and draw valid conclusions. All this is only truly realised, however, when one uses pedagogic processes which 'deliberately bring the thinking to the surface, to make it visible'.

MAKING THINKING VISIBLE IN...
MFL
BY CHERRY BAILEY

(with specific reference to German)

The expert disciplinary thinking process I have chosen to focus on with regards to the learning of modern foreign languages (MFL) is much more aligned to mathematical problem-solving rather than, ironically, the reading model outlined in Collins et al.'s 'Cognitive Apprenticeship' paper.

In the MFL classroom, it is reading that students often find particularly challenging, especially with German, where students frequently encounter fewer cognates as they encounter more complex language, and word order can throw them off course if they do not think strategically.

By 'reading skills', I mean the specific skills required to enable students to gain a full understanding of a complete text, which contains vocabulary and grammatical structures beyond those which students have been formally taught. Research has shown that students need to know 95% of the vocabulary in a text in order to be able to comprehend it (Schmitt et al., 2011).

The reality is, however, that the vast majority of students are faced with texts which contain a significant proportion of unknown words. If we simply focus on developing skills in answering exam-style comprehension questions, we waste the opportunity for students to pick up the full range of language offered in a text, and they will resort to pure guesswork in exams, based on individual words they recognise, rather than 'thinking like a linguist' and using problem-solving skills to extract key information.

By teaching students how to treat a text as a complex problem-solving task and using the cognitive apprenticeship process of modelling, scaffolding, coaching, and fading, we can enable students to not only tackle such texts with confidence but also in the process extend and embed their knowledge and understanding of the language they are learning.

If students can develop problem-solving cognitive strategies which enable them to integrate and apply the skills and knowledge they have acquired in the course of MFL teaching to new and challenging situations, they will maximise the impact of the limited exposure they have had to the language in question.

Teaching the thinking process is not something that can be done in just a few lessons: there is no quick fix. As with all aspects of language teaching, it is a case of introducing new skills and knowledge bit by bit, and continually revisiting, interleaving and practising them within the normal course of teaching new material.

It is, however, important that students do not simply practise these subskills in isolation – they need to have a conceptual model of the whole. For this reason, we start every new topic throughout KS3 and KS4 with a full text incorporating some known (but also a lot of new) vocabulary and grammar (as Collins et al. say, 'global skills before local') and do not shy away from tackling whole texts in the normal course of teaching.

In addition to the domain knowledge – the new vocabulary and grammatical structures taught each lesson – it is necessary to explicitly model heuristic strategies, the 'generally effective techniques and approaches for accomplishing tasks that might be regarded as "tricks of the trade"'. Examples include the following:

- Making unconscious knowledge of English grammar conscious

- Identifying the role played by particular words in a sentence, through using knowledge of word order, use of capital letters, endings on words

- Breaking down words into component parts to work out meaning

- Thinking of other German words they already know that contain part of the word

- Drawing comparisons with English vocabulary and grammar

- Using logic to guess and then verify possible meanings

- Not glossing over 'little words' which may actually negate or contradict any meaning they have already worked out

- Being aware that they may need to read the whole sentence – and beyond – before they can understand the first word

- Accepting that sometimes they may have to move on with gaps in knowledge, but they may be able to fill those gaps once they have completed the whole task

Modelling and Scaffolding

It is better to avoid lengthy explanations of the thinking process in a mixed prior attainment, mixed motivation class. Instead, involve the class in the modelling process by scaffolding it: ask *them* the questions that you would instinctively go through in your head to prompt them to 'solve' a word, such as *stundenlang* in the extract below.

> *Seitdem ich in der neunten Klasse bin, setze ich mich **stundenlang** an den Computer zu Hause und mache nie meine alten Hobbys wie Tennis und Schwimmen.*

For example, can they see which two words this compound word is made of? Do they know the meanings of either word? Any wrong answers are often useful pointers to further understanding both the process and the domain knowledge. If somebody guesses a meaning for the word that cannot be correct because it plays a different grammatical role, ask if anyone can see why that can't be right. Usually someone will be able to point out, for example, that it can't be a noun because it doesn't have a capital letter, or it can't be a verb because either it doesn't have a verb ending or is in the wrong place in the sentence. They should all know that *lang* means 'long'. *Stunde* they will more likely remember as 'lesson' rather than 'hour'. If they want to try it meaning 'lesson', ask further questions about the context to see if it works. They will soon realise that Stunde must have another meaning as it doesn't make any sense. So get them to work out more of the sentence. They can't ignore the little word 'nie' because it is pretty key to understanding the scenario – that the writer 'never' does their old hobbies. Ask what kind of a word *setze* is: as it accompanies the *ich* and ends in an 'e', they should recognise it as a verb. Get them to sound it out in the context and pretty quickly they realise it means 'I sit' at the computer. Even if no one remembers that *Stunde* also means 'hour', once they have solved all parts of the equation ('They sit at the computer long *something* and never do their old hobbies'), they should quickly work out that it means 'for a long time' – or 'for hours'.

The process of modelling the thinking process allows us to teach 'control strategies', to decide alternative courses of action to solve the problem. Without guidance, students tend to fall back on the most common default position, which is to focus on one word they think looks like it might be a cognate or near cognate and use that as a basis for the whole translation/reading comprehension task. The visible thinking process also leads to students retaining any new domain knowledge far more effectively: they are far more likely to remember all of the new words they had to analyse in a variety of ways than if they had simply answered a comprehension question on a text.

Coaching

When students have sufficient domain knowledge and awareness of the heuristic strategies, you can coach them to go through the process independently. Generally I find it works best in cooperation between either pairs or small mixed prior attainment groups, as, even with regular practice, some weaker students find it difficult to manage on their own, while more able students can extend their own apprenticeship by having to articulate their thought processes. Weaker students may need additional support, such as the provision of key vocabulary which they have been taught but may not remember, as well as more intervention and guidance as to which strategy to try next.

Each small group or pair has their own extract from a text they have to work out and feed back to the rest of the class – including how they worked out the meanings of unknown words. I rarely if ever simply give them the meaning of a word they don't know: I will ask them questions to get them to work it out for themselves.

The eureka moments come when you hear students asking each other the questions I would ask them, or explaining why a particular suggestion can't be right (articulation).

Fading

The extent to which I can fade will vary from pupil to pupil: some will become very confident very quickly; others will need significant scaffolding and coaching throughout their time learning the language – and that is fine, because even if they do not fully 'pass' the cognitive apprenticeship by the time they take their GCSE, their knowledge of the language, and confidence to use it, will be considerably greater than if they had not experienced it. Pupils who do become proficient at the apprenticeship thinking model will not only do better in the language they are learning but also be in a good position to learn any other languages they may wish – or need – to learn in the future.

PSYCHOLOGY

BY JULIE KETTLEWELL

When I first started considering what characterises a great psychology student, I came up with a relatively long list; however, one expert disciplinary thinking process stood out as being the most significant.

Students who are really successful in our subject are able to think critically about evidence, considering strengths and limitations, which enables them to draw sound conclusions. They are able to use this evaluation to make comparisons between different types of research method: for example, explaining that case studies have a small sample size, making them less likely to be representative of the general population, whereas experiments based on large groups of people are more likely to lead to findings that are generalisable. They are also able to use their evaluation of different theories to make comparisons between the various approaches in psychology: for example, explaining that the biological approach is deterministic and ignores the role of free will, whereas the cognitive approach recognises that we do have control over our decision making and therefore is able to account for the success of therapies such as cognitive behavioural therapy.

This is a critical thinking process; however, it is a complex skill as it requires the students to develop this skill of evaluation and comparison. Those students who just try to rote learn answers without truly understanding these concepts are easy to identify, both in discussions with them and when reading their work. Furthermore, the skill of critiquing research and the skill of making comparisons (not just describing one piece of research and then moving on to describe the other) are processes that experts develop in psychology and need to be taught to novices explicitly.

When teaching these skills, I consciously aim to make my thinking process visible to the students in ways which resonate with the processes Collins et al. outline in their paper 'Cognitive Apprenticeship'.

One way I do this is by following the seven-step model outlined in the Education Endowment Foundation's *Metacognition and Self-Regulated Learning* guidance report (Quigley et al., 2018). The purpose of these steps is to shift the responsibility from the teacher to the students, and the teacher moves from being the coach to being a supportive and sympathetic audience.

1. **Activating prior knowledge**
   At this stage, I establish if students have sufficient background knowledge in order to undertake analysis and make comparisons. Sometimes I make this entirely teacher-led, whereas other times I do it as a quiz. Whichever format it takes, the key element is addressing gaps in knowledge before moving on. For example, if students are going to be comparing theories using some new terminology, first we will spend time ensuring they definitely understand the key concepts of these theories.

2. **Explicit strategy instruction**
   At this point, I provide students with question stems to help students write a comparison. These will help them to consider similarities and differences and to use key terminology that they should include in their comparisons.

3. **Modelling of learned strategy**
   I will now use multiple models. Initially I model by thinking aloud and, using the visualiser, I will talk as I write my example comparison, which the students will also write down in their notes. The amount I model gradually diminishes as the students take on more responsibility. I will continue to model any parts of the process that students struggle with and will call upon more capable students to provide the modelling here for their peers.

4. **Memorisation of strategy**
   Questioning is critical here and at this point I will do a quiz and use whiteboards to check all of the class has understood. I will ensure the quiz questions allow misconceptions to be addressed.

5. **Guided practice**
   The 'Guided practice' step is of particular importance, and I ensure that I spend sufficient time on this stage. I will start with easier comparisons and build up to more complex ones. Initially, students will observe, enact and practise making comparisons with help from other students, but gradually the difficulty of the task increases. This stage will include teacher guided practice, reciprocal teaching and small group work. If necessary, students can refer back to the question stems given to them in step 2 to help them with writing a comparison.

6. **Independent practice**

Students are given several analysis tasks to complete by themselves. This stage is essential so that the skill of analysing and comparing becomes automatic. I deliberately provide them with extensive practice as this decontextualises the learning so the strategies can be applied to novel situations.

7. **Structured reflection**

I work with students and explicitly show them how to do this. They have the chance to look over their work, review what was learned, and see the bigger picture. I also provide them with questions to enable them to reflect on themselves as a learner.

This reflects the detail of the 'Cognitive Apprenticeship' paper as students see the processes of the work and see the strategies that experts use when they are undertaking such complex tasks. It addresses the four processes of cognitive apprenticeship: modelling, scaffolding, fading and coaching.

Modelling is done in various ways in stage 3, but these all aim to expose the students to how the expert would perform the task. This enables them to 'build a conceptual model of the processes that are required to accomplish it'.

The seven-step model is a scaffolding framework that provides a temporary and adjustable support for students. Collins et al.'s paper claims that 'a requisite to such scaffolding is accurate diagnosis of the student's current skill level or difficulty and the availability of an intermediate step at the appropriate level of difficulty in carrying out the target activity'. This is why I check for misconceptions in stage 4 and continually monitor the students while they carry out guided practice.

Fading involves the gradual removal of supports until students are on their own. This happens incrementally as we move through the seven stages.

Coaching occurs throughout the process in order to 'direct the students' attention to a previously unnoticed aspect of the task or simply to remind the student of some aspect of the task that is known but has been temporarily overlooked'.

The aim is to help students generalise this skill so that they can transfer it when faced with novel situations, e.g. research methods or approaches that they have not previously critically compared.

Dimension Three

SEQUENCING
Keys to ordering learning activities

When it comes to sequencing activities, Collins et al. insist that you **begin globally** before looking at local skills. This gives the learner a 'conceptual map … before attending to the details of the terrain'. Tasks must be sequenced to ensure an **increase in complexity** and then teachers must **diversify** tasks, to help students explore the breadth and depth of the subject domain.

SEQUENCING
Keys to ordering learning activities

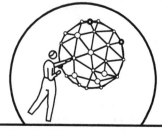

GLOBAL BEFORE LOCAL SKILLS
Focus on conceptualizing the whole
task before executing the parts

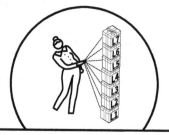

INCREASING COMPLEXITY
Meaningful tasks gradually
increasing in difficulty

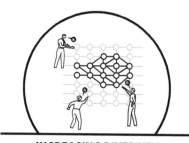

INCREASING DIVERSITY
Practice in a variety of situations to
emphasize broad application

A summary introduction to Dimension Three:
SEQUENCING

Chemists Penny Holland and Alister Talbot promote Collins et al.'s mantra, 'global before local'. They ensure students learn the basics of atomic structure so that the students can apply that knowledge to a range of different problems. And they begin with the big picture, which 'shows them what they're aiming for, which can be important in a subject that can be abstract for students'.

Challenging my colleagues to think hard about the cognitive processes inherent in their individual disciplines was fun, and never more so than with Garry Littlewood. Thinking like a chef requires an attention to the 'details of the terrain' like no other subject. He makes visible the unconscious competence inherent in the cooking process. If you cook yourself and want to know what thinking processes you are undertaking subliminally whilst you're making white sauce, then you are in for a treat!

Deputy headteacher Matt Smith's chapter on mathematical thinking is a masterclass in sequencing the complexity of tasks to surface and then develop expert disciplinary thought. He explores how to set up tasks which are incrementally more challenging through variation theory. Watching Matt teach low prior attainment learners with patient persistence, you see how he anticipates students' logical but erroneous thinking processes. Indeed, he reflects here upon how he is still surprised 'that many students do not recognise that $5x + 3 = 13$ and $13 = 5x + 3$ are the same question!'

Similarly to Matt Smith, our subject leader of media studies, Karl Elwell, explains with utter clarity how establishing a thinking toolkit for analysing media texts is crucial before he makes 'visible exactly how we can use these tools to deconstruct increasingly diverse and challenging texts, whether they are still or moving image'. Karl's account of how he teaches the expert thinking processes of a media analyst could have been included in any of the four dimensions, but I sited it here because he is very clear about how important it is to teach the fundamental thinking processes thoroughly before progressing onto more varied texts.

Nigel Currie unpicks the humble forward roll to great effect! As he makes clear in the final chapter of this sequencing section, 'it is crucial in physical education to teach the basic motor skills in a way that enables a student to apply their strategic knowledge in a progressively expert fashion under the increasing pressure of performance'. Here Nigel provides us with a lucid exposition of how he verbalises what he is thinking as he executes the most basic of physical activities, and holds this up as a model for making thinking visible across the whole PE curriculum.

CHEMISTRY

BY PENNY HOLLAND & ALISTER TALBOT

'Even in domains that rest on elaborate conceptual and factual underpinnings, students must learn the practice or art of solving problems.'

Chemistry is a subject based upon conceptual and factual knowledge. Ask a class of year 7 science students to draw an atom and the most common response would be simply a circle; they haven't yet been taught the conceptual and factual knowledge necessary to attempt this task with any scientific accuracy or meaning.

A chemistry teacher obviously needs to communicate to students a sound grasp of this conceptual and factual subject specific knowledge. But, as Collins et al. point out in their 'Cognitive Apprenticeship' paper, 'this kind of knowledge, although certainly important, provides insufficient clues for many students about how to solve problems and accomplish tasks in a domain'.

It is possible to teach the key knowledge of chemistry as discrete topics such as atomic structure, the periodic table and chemical reactions, requiring students to memorise the rules and trends verbatim. Alternatively, we propose that an expert chemistry teacher would prioritise a deeper understanding of these core foundational principles, making explicit links between them to allow students to apply their knowledge and understanding to make deductions.

Expert chemistry teachers will teach their students to apply their knowledge of atomic structure to predict and therefore explain the reactivity trend of group 1. Furthermore, the expert chemistry teacher would encourage students to reflect on the rules and strategies they employed, to apply to further novel contexts.

We believe that the approach we propose is fundamental to being an expert chemistry teacher and developing the ability of students to think like a chemist.

Sticking with atomic structure, securing the conceptual and factual knowledge requires some deliberate planning. Even at this stage, the four stages of the cognitive apprenticeship process – modelling, scaffolding, fading, coaching – are essential pedagogic practice:

1. **Identification of the core foundational principles:** for example, atomic structure, the periodic table, chemical reactions

2. **Sequencing the learning of these principles to build up these big ideas:** for example, you wouldn't teach reactivity of group 1 before atomic structure. Each principle then requires dissection to determine the key knowledge and component skills, to identify a starting point and a logical order in which to work through e.g. covering subatomic particles before the definitions of proton and mass number.

3. **Setting up the learning by showing students the big picture or end goal:** for example, a complete dot and cross diagram of a model of an atom. This shows them what they're aiming for, which is often important in a subject that can be abstract for students, and also serves to highlight the skills and knowledge they need to acquire in order to be able to complete the task.

4. **Teaching and learning cycle of explanation, modelling, scaffolding and SLOP (shed loads of practice!) for key knowledge/each component skill:** for example, when teaching atomic structure, an explanation of the structure of the atom, subatomic particles and definitions of mass and proton number, followed by teacher *modelling* of how to work out the number of subatomic particles for a particular element using the mass and proton numbers from the periodic table. Students then practise this skill with *scaffolded* support from the teacher which is then reduced or *faded*. As per Christodoulou's 'embedding of component skills' (Christodoulou, 2017), the teacher would not move onto the next skill (e.g. electron arrangement) until the previous step had been secured, building up to the student being able to piece together the component skills to complete the overall task. Further practice with *coaching* support from the teacher improves fluency so that many of these more basic component skills become automatic, and revisiting these key skills and concepts regularly prevents forgetting.

As Collins et al. highlight, this 'involves an expert's performing a task so that the students can observe and build a conceptual model of the processes that are required to accomplish it. In cognitive domains, this requires the externalization of usually internal processes and activities – specifically, the heuristics and control processes by which experts apply their basic conceptual and procedural knowledge.' Making explicit links between these key ideas to apply to problem-solving is the next stage of cognitive apprenticeship teaching.

For students to apply their knowledge to problem-solve initially requires the chemistry teacher to articulate their own thinking when approaching a problem. For example, take the GCSE examination question about the reactivity of group 1: 'State and explain the trend in reactivity of group 1 elements in terms of atomic structure.'

It is suggested that teacher modelling should be done with students understanding that they will soon be tackling a similar problem to the one you model. An expert chemist would be able to deduce and explain the trend using core principles. 'The teacher's thinking must be made visible to the students' and an expert chemist would think as follows:

1. From my understanding of atomic structure, I know that:

    • All elements in group 1 have one electron on their outer electron shell and that these atoms are unstable as they do not have a full outer shell of electrons.

    • As you go down group 1, the atoms get larger, as more shells of electrons are added.

2. From my understanding of chemical reactions, I know that group 1 elements react by losing an electron from their outer shell.

3. Thus a link can be made between these two topic areas – an electron will be more easily lost from a larger atom.

4. An expert chemist would ask themselves, 'Why is this?' and would remember the fact that electrons are negatively charged, and protons which are located in the nucleus are positively charged. Therefore, there will be an attraction between the outer electron and the nucleus.

5. The chemist would then link this back to the idea from atomic structure that in a larger atom, this attraction will be weaker, the electron will be lost more easily and the reactivity would increase going down the group.

On first inspection, this may appear more complex than simply memorising the answer to the question, but in reality, an expert chemist only needs to have two pieces of knowledge to tackle this question which can be applied to novel contexts, and we would argue this is much more effective than being taught to learn the trend in group 1 reactivity by rote.

An expert teacher would provide further opportunities for students to practise following the teacher *modelling*, and would support as a *coach* by eliciting from the students the thinking processes they are going through. 'The goal is to help students generalize the skill, to learn when the skill is or is not applicable, and to transfer the skill independently when faced with novel situations', and although Collins et al. propose that it is the foundational domains of reading, writing and mathematics that engage metacognitive processes, in our experience as chemistry teachers in a subject such as ours, which is conceptually and factually dense, students can be taught, through teacher modelling of the expert thinking processes, how to apply their knowledge to problem-solving tasks as self-regulated learners.

MAKING THINKING VISIBLE IN...

FOOD

BY GARRY LITTLEWOOD

Throughout my teaching career, many colleagues have said 'I love cooking and it would be great to teach a food lesson.' After observing me teach, the same colleagues never again express the desire to teach a food lesson! They leave the classroom astonished at what it takes for twenty students to plan and make a dish successfully, and then evaluate their own performance. My colleagues readily acknowledge that there is so much more involved than 'just cooking'.

The question is, how do students develop from complete kitchen novices to independent, expert practitioners? As you will see, the cognitive apprenticeship model described by Collins et al. has enabled me to articulate that process.

Unpicking how students develop from novices to experts is complex. Cooking can be described as a blend of science and art. Before a student can develop into an expert food practitioner, knowledge needs to be gained, techniques and skills need to be learned, and control involving planning, evaluation and correction needs to be mastered.

An expert food teacher teaches students to 'think like a cook' rather than just teaching students 'how to cook'.

To begin with, students must be taught the knowledge and genuine understanding of the working properties of ingredients, in addition to their nutritional properties. Without this knowledge and understanding, students do not have the tools to think. If, halfway through a recipe, the raw ingredients are not reacting as anticipated, then unless a student knows and understands the working properties of those ingredients, it is impossible to respond in time to save things.

There is a disciplinary principle which underpins all successful food teaching: 'Think like a scientist and demonstrate like an artist.' It is perhaps more explicitly expressed in the following phrase (which sounds like a Chinese proverb): 'Rescue a lumpy sauce to send a student home with a decent macaroni cheese; teach a student about gelatinisation and they'll make perfect sauces for life!' This is because when they understand the process – what is actually happening to the ingredients when the sauce begins to go lumpy – they can intervene and eradicate the lumps in any sauce they might be making.

To explain this disciplinary principle in more detail, the GCSE course is designed around food science and nutrition topics that are taught with related practical work. Before meringues are made, the functional properties of protein and scientific principles are studied; once you understand the disruptive effect of fat on foams, you are far more likely to take the trouble to wash your bowl before you start to whisk and thus avoid getting egg yolk in with the whites!

When John Tomsett challenged me to explain what is unique about expert thinking in food teaching, after much robust dialogue with him I eventually settled upon three elements of thinking which, combined, comprise the cognitive processes of the expert foodie! If you think like an expert food practitioner you must do the following:

1. **Stay three steps ahead.** Cooks need to be thinking at all times, anticipating all the hurdles which could derail the cooking process. We need to teach students to think this way by articulating such thinking in real time. Being able to multitask is crucial on a student's path to being successful in the food classroom. Making this real-time thinking visible is the key to students becoming expert foodies. In my classroom, I do this by constantly verbalising, demonstrating and modelling my own thinking processes.

2. **Understand the sensory profile required to monitor and evaluate the process almost subliminally.** Having a trained eye, tongue and nose to constantly analyse, question and evaluate is essential. Following a recipe involves dovetailing tasks, building in checks and monitoring with corrective action. This sensory thinking is done whilst actually cooking, and occurs simultaneously with the cook's cognitive thinking.

3. **Apply knowledge and understanding of the ingredients** to comprehend in seconds what your eyes, tongue and nose are telling you about what is happening to your ingredients, so that you can intervene in time before it is too late and you end up pouring your dish into the food recycling bin.

In summary, whilst you are cooking, you need to **think procedurally three steps** ahead (the oven needs to warm before you put in your pasta bake in cheese sauce, and the pasta pan needs to be on the boil), **use your eyes, tongue and nose to monitor what is happening to your ingredients** (the flour has lumped together and it smells like the milk is burning) and **apply your knowledge and understanding of your ingredients** (now you have turned the heat down, you need to stir the colloidal suspension more vigorously or else more lumps will form during gelatinisation).

It is important to emphasise that this thinking can only happen if it is underpinned by thorough disciplinary knowledge and understanding at every stage.

Making these three elements of the expert food practitioner's thinking process explicit by modelling and scaffolding in real-time helps develop novices into experts, gradually taking away the scaffolds as mastery of the students' thinking processes develop.

Collins et al. define cognitive apprenticeship as 'a model of instruction that works to make thinking visible'. Providing well-planned demonstrations – which emphasise talking through what is going on in the demonstrator's head – is a powerful method to make thinking visible.

A thoroughly planned, highly effective demonstration:

- articulates the food teacher's three-steps ahead thinking ('Before I begin, I need to check the date on the milk and that the oven gloves are out and to turn the oven on to 180°C...');

- contains scientific explanations of *how* and *why* ingredients work together ('Remember, flour provides the **starch** that becomes thickened in the gelatinisation process, within which milk provides the necessary **moisture** and the hob's **heat** helps the temporary suspension become permanent...');

- includes crafted/planned questions for students at crucial stages of the demonstration ('What else will I need to do in two minutes to prevent this soufflé going saggy in the middle? Why?');

- provides the clear visualisation of skills and processes ('Here, watch carefully how I make sure that my spatula gets beneath the *whole* omelette before I slide it onto the plate');

- verbalises what is seen, tasted and smelt diagnostically ('Well, that mint is very strong, so I will just use two crushed leaves now and I will remember to taste-check later if I need more').

At key stage 3, we begin by giving students simple schemas to enable them to be independent cooks; but as students progress to GCSE, we expect them to take control and begin the 'fade' stage to think like cooks for themselves. Food teachers implicitly teach the four aspects of traditional apprenticeship:

modelling, scaffolding, fading and coaching through well-planned and -sequenced schemas.

Until I discovered Collins et al.'s paper, I found it difficult to articulate how we teach students to cook. But the principles of cognitive apprenticeship provided me with the framework to explain in tangible terms how food teachers seemingly sprinkle magic dust over a year 7 student who has had little experience of cooking – maybe making rice crispy cakes with grandparents – and transform the student into an independent, confident and increasingly expert cook who can make three complex dishes for their GCSE practical examination.

I once observed a mathematics lesson on expanding brackets. The mathematics teacher wrote the following five questions on the board and the students were completing them in their exercise books:

1. $5(a + 3)$

2. $4(b + 2)$

3. $3(f + 2)$

4. $2(g + 7)$

5. $7(t + 9)$

To hurry them along, the teacher announced, 'I want you to do these questions to the point where you don't even need to think about them!' Of course, this proved quite easy – the hardest *thinking* arguably being the multiplication of 7 and 9.

For me, this is the knife-edge moment when teaching mathematics; of course practice is important – it builds fluency and confidence – but if we are not careful, we can ignore the crucial mathematical structures that exist within our subject and provide the key to genuine understanding.

Students who practise questions to the point that they 'don't even need to think about them' are in grave danger of being unable to apply what they know because they do not understand the disciplinary thinking behind the mathematics. The expert's thought processes remain invisible, hidden behind an impenetrable wall of false competence.

It is important for mathematics teachers to invest time in exploring structure before any type of practice takes place. Within seconds, I could 'teach' a student how to do the questions like the ones above, but if my question 6 was '**Expand** $-5(-3 - 2x)$' then my teaching would be exposed as being ineffective and superficial.

I would argue that the explicit teaching of mathematical structure – especially when working with algebra – is the expert disciplinary thinking process that classroom practitioners need to be able to make visible when teaching mathematics. An ineffective teacher will focus too much of their time on methods at the expense of examining the many structural forms of mathematics which support true understanding. (I believe teaching methods is important, by the way, it's just that they are insufficient on their own.)

Let's re-examine the topic of expanding brackets again.

Expand 5(a + 3)

What does the above question mean? What structure do we see? What do we need to do?

Our first step is to think about some of the mathematical understanding that underpins this question. Understanding the *order of operations* (sometimes unhelpfully referred to as BIDMAS) is an important stage here. We can see an addition [**3** is being added to **a**] and we can hopefully appreciate that this *addition* is being multiplied by 5 (as the addition is in brackets). This simple structure is really key to understanding the question and needs to be made explicit when teaching. A simple technique that seems to work is to ask the students what they see, as you can then start to unpick what structures they are observing for themselves.

There are also some important multiplicative structures that are vital to understanding this question. Understanding that 23×9 is the same as 20×9 added to 3×9 is a really key component of the structural element to the question.

So, the cognitive thinking here is all about *structure*. As Collins et al. claim, teachers need to model this type of thinking explicitly to students. I make the thinking visible by really spelling out the key structures in all mathematics that we encounter. I scaffold their thinking: sometimes I will take the opportunity to talk to them about structure; other times, I will ask them 'What can you see?' The latter can be incredibly revealing and helpful, especially when correcting misconceptions.

Furthermore, I think it is important to build up the conceptual model. Once the students have understood the concept and structure of 5(a + 3), just look at how we can tweak the question:

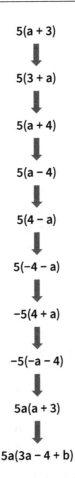

$5(a + 3)$

$5(3 + a)$

$5(a + 4)$

$5(a - 4)$

$5(4 - a)$

$5(-4 - a)$

$-5(4 + a)$

$-5(-a - 4)$

$5a(a + 3)$

$5a(3a - 4 + b)$

This is where some students can struggle with mathematics. I once came across a student who was completing a practice GCSE paper. One of the questions was: *Expand 4(x − 3)*. He did this without any trouble at all. The next question was: *Expand (and simplify): 4(e + 3) + 2(e − 4)*. He didn't even attempt the question. The change of structure had flummoxed him; he couldn't break down the structural elements of the question. He was a student who relied on a specific method for a specific type of structure, without having any appreciation of what made the structure unique or how the structure could change.

Variation theory is a useful pedagogical component when exploring mathematical structure. Put simply, it is the creation of sequences and behaviour to enable mathematical thinking in the classroom. The above chain of questions on expanding brackets has been sequenced carefully so that learners can detect small changes in the behaviour of the question but where the structure of the questions remains intact. It is a really effective strategy that, when implemented effectively, can reinforce the key thinking that students need to undertake when exploring mathematical structure.

I would argue that expert mathematical thinking is all about recognising and understanding structure, especially algebraic and multiplicative structures. The key challenge is finding ways to get students to think like this! These are my suggestions and strategies:

- When teaching new concepts, focus explicitly on structure.

- Ask the question 'What can you see?' This really encourages learners to examine and explore mathematical structure for themselves. In 17 years of teaching, it still surprises me that many students do not recognise that '5x + 3 = 13' and '13 = 5x + 3' are the same question!

- Use variation theory in your planning to tweak the look of a question, but ensure that the mathematical structures remain the same. The website *Increasingly Difficult Questions* (www.bit.ly/3okH13d) does this really well. I have used sets of questions from that site many times with my classes; they always reveal something interesting and get me to really focus on explicitly modelling structure before teaching.

- Once the students have understood the structure, allow them to practise different methods, varying the structures, to gain fluency of thinking.

Having instilled in your learners an appreciation of mathematical structure, you will find that they apply a whole new way of thinking that allows them to be more expert mathematicians. As Collins et al. point out, 'To students, learning mathematics had meant learning a set of mathematical operations and methods. [Cognitive apprenticeship entails] teaching students that doing mathematics consists not only in applying problem-solving procedures but in reasoning about and managing problems.'

MAKING THINKING VISIBLE IN...
MEDIA STUDIES
BY KARL ELWELL

A world of 24/7 open media is the only one that our students, as 'digital natives', have ever known. One of the most vital aspects of media studies is developing a student's ability to understand that all media texts are *constructions* and educating them to analyse media texts rather than just consume them. The thinking processes behind effective textual analysis is fundamental to media studies.

What we are hoping to achieve from our students, ultimately, is critical autonomy in their textual analysis. This is where a student is able to see through the mist of subjectivity that surrounds a media text and is able to comment not only on *how* the text has been constructed but more importantly *why* it has been constructed in that way. This is a key objective and comes after time spent building an understanding of media representations, audiences, industries and of course the contexts that surround them.

The way into this type of student thinking, though, begins with changing the mindset of students who come into the classroom ready to *describe* what they see but not automatically thinking beyond what immediate gratification the media text provides for them. Teaching that thinking process, through which students start to develop a critical understanding of texts and in so doing develop their own analytical eye, is fundamental to the subject. It is the starting point through which students deconstruct texts and therefore realise that they are in fact constructions – and that they are constructed in that way for a specific purpose.

This is where other key aspects of media studies become connected and students move through the course and start to appreciate, and begin to comment upon, the influence of the underlying thread: media language – representation – audience – industry – contexts. This is why, at this 'launch point', students need clarity in the way in which they learn and are able to fully replicate the thinking processes that we, as experts, illustrate within the classroom.

The time spent teaching the textual analysis of media texts comes early in the course but begins only after students have a basic understanding of media terminology. This provides them with the technical language that they will use to decode texts and enhances their confidence in the subject. The next steps are making visible exactly how we can use these tools to deconstruct increasingly diverse and challenging texts, whether they are still or moving images. This stage and those that follow are closely aligned with the detail in Collins et al.'s 'Cognitive Apprenticeship' paper.

One of the key early exercises in teaching textual analysis is to simply annotate an image projected onto a board at the front of the class. As a teacher, one labels the components that have been used in the construction of that media product – for example, a magazine front cover. So here we are applying all of the terminology for that particular type of text; in the magazine's case, the masthead, cover lines, strap line, etc. It is important that you talk through this process and show the class how these separate components are working together. Students can then do the same with their own examples – noting that they must use the technical terminology they have learnt.

The next stage for me to **model** is the *effect* of each of the components used in the construction of the product that we have labelled. So, for example, we might have labelled a low angle shot, but why has the shot been taken in that way? Are the producers trying to make this person look more powerful? Here debate is encouraged and we begin to entice answers out of students who naturally begin to connect the concepts linked to representation, audience and industries.

As well as what I am thinking, it is really important to know what the students are thinking, and the next stage is for the students to take the role of 'teacher'. With another shared example, students lead the activity and the board becomes full of interconnected ideas. As Collins et al. note, 'by bringing these tacit processes into the open, students can observe, enact, and practice them with help from the teacher and from other students'. This process helps students to realise that the media is an industry and is trying to manipulate the audience in some way. There are excellent opportunities available here to discuss how different producers of the text 'think' and how and why the example they are deconstructing is the way that it is, or how it could be different. Students are placed in the role of producers and are encouraged to think in that way.

The exercise culminates in writing a textual analysis and here **scaffolding** helps all learners. The students have proven that they know how a text might be put together but writing an analysis of an unseen text, in exam conditions, is a requirement of any GCSE or A level course and therefore it is a skill that they must master. I begin with a table of two columns and the headings will simply be 'technique' and 'effect' – students need to populate it with each media language technique that has been used in the creation of the text on one side and then explain the effect that it has on the other.

Again I **model** an example first, explaining my own ideas and justifying my thinking aloud. They are moving from description to analysis – from 'how it is' to 'why it is that way' – and it is important that they understand this. This activity helps them to organise their ideas and I encourage them to add the terms 'signifier'/'signified' and 'denotation'/'connotation' to any verbal feedback they give when they articulate their answers to the class. Challenging each other is really important as they begin to explore alternative 'readings' and explain their own thoughts with specific examples from the text.

Drawing these simple ideas together, I model how to write their observations into analyses. We work on what makes a good answer and analyse sample paragraphs as a class, with me providing the voice and thoughts of an 'examiner', explaining what the 'expert' would be looking for in a good answer. This is akin to early **coaching** but initially very much at whole-class level.

The support given is **faded**, as the students grow in confidence and obtain greater autonomy in their analyses. We move onto the analysis of moving image texts where I make visible my thinking in a shared, class textual analysis, but I expect more reflection from students, hoping that they challenge other people's reading of the text, including mine. I ask questions of the students and test their understanding, hoping that through this they develop their own answers.

Students are then **coached** further in their writing. They are given feedback to refine their written analyses before moving to independent practice. This sees them analyse a range of different texts, of various genres and mediums. This 'exploration' is encouraged through the students working independently, away from the classroom, and sees them setting their own questions/tasks. This process becomes easier as we move through the course and students explore the importance of context. We **coach** students at an individual level, developing their written analyses, as they become increasingly proficient in being able to explain why a text is the way that it is.

Through the whole teaching of textual analysis, we are constantly building confidence in our learners. By verbalising our approach as experts at each stage, our thinking is made visible to the students; consequently, with practice, they develop an embedded understanding of how they themselves should, thought by thought, cognitively deconstruct any media text.

PHYSICAL EDUCATION

BY NIGEL CURRIE

Ultimately my aim as a teacher of performance-based physical education is to move a novice learner from an isolated skill-based scenario through to a position where they can perform in a strategic fashion; for example, from a start point of stopping and sending a hockey ball to selecting the correct pass under the pressure of a dynamic and competitive game situation.

I need to provide the support that moves my learner from a cognitive stage (big picture understanding of what is required), through an associative phase (trial and error), to arrive at the autonomous destination (able to perform without having to think about how to execute those basic motor skills). In essence, if this is successful, they will have undertaken the process of Collins et al.'s cognitive apprenticeship in physical education.

Take the example of teaching a gymnastic routine. First of all the student requires a representation of what a good routine could look like as a final performance. This 'big picture' stage is crucial; too often there is an assumption in physical education that students know what an expert performance looks like. In reality, the vast majority of students will not have seen an expert modelling a gymnastic routine, or a driven dribble lay-up in basketball, or the controlling of a short pass followed by a reverse stick pass that spreads the play in hockey.

Having seen the potential end point of the learning, the next step is to drill down into the basic elements with lots of explicitly articulated support.

An example of teaching the basics would be looking at how we travel within a gymnastic routine. This requires, amongst other elements, the perfecting of a forward roll. Here modelling and scaffolding become key. In the instance of the forward roll, the scaffolding can actually become physical: a springboard under a gym mat can aid the novice in gaining the momentum required to roll.

As with any scaffolding, physical or verbal, this can be removed as the gymnast moves from apprentice towards mastery of the skill. I can use this phase to articulate my thinking as I, or an expert student, demonstrates a model forward roll. Through commentary or narration alongside the performance of the skill in focus, I am able to highlight key technical points, allay fears and address common misconceptions/errors 'live'. This format of prompts is powerful and explicit in making my thinking visible, allowing the inner expert in me to share and demonstrate to students how to approach the skill in their mind.

This process can be repeated throughout the teaching of the core skills required to compile a gymnastic routine. Procedural supports or interventions can be used to move the student along the gymnastic continuum from novice towards expert.

As my physical education learner moves from the cognitive towards the associative stage of learning, I can remove scaffold but do not take it away entirely, as they could fall flat on their face (metaphorically and physically). As understanding and ability increases in the basic gymnastic skills with my support, greater emphasis can be applied to the planning/choreography and aesthetics of the gymnastic routine. This will require a revisit to the initial 'bigger picture' of the expert modelled routine and an increasingly collaborative approach.

A hugely helpful factor in the design and refinement of the routine is enabling students the 'opportunities for reflection on their own and other's efforts'. Scardamalia et al. (1984) developed an approach towards the teaching of writing that included these windows for sharing and reflection between students. Building in periodic pauses that allow students to critique the work of their peers is a lesson staple, enabling students to take those first steps in articulating their embryonic expert thinking. The social characteristics of the learning environment are important.

Within a typical gymnastics class, you will have a range of abilities and experiences, no different to the apprentice car mechanic working alongside a master technician. If harnessed correctly, this social mix can be a great aid to independent learner development.

Scardamalia et al. also included procedural prompts that reduced cognitive overload or the information processing burden for students in their writing. In a similar way, the design of a gymnastic routine includes 'planning cues' that enable the students to join together the core gymnastic skills in a way that creates the routine that was initially modelled. These prompts, in the case of students working independently on their gymnastic routine, are the required elements of the routine outlined on a whiteboard in the gymnasium. It acts as a heuristic that aids the planning of the routine through a checklist of ingredients. This simple procedural prompt can enable the learner, through exploration, to apply their core gymnastic skills in an expert way.

In effect, I have articulated or illustrated my thinking as to how I would design a gymnastic routine in a format that is quickly referenced and cognitively unrestrictive for the student.

It is crucial in physical education to teach the basic motor skills of something as simple as a forward roll in a way that enables a student to apply their strategic knowledge in a progressively expert fashion under the increasing pressure of performance. In establishing the optimum environment for the successful apprentice in physical education, sequencing is particularly key. As Collins et al. suggest:

- Within sequencing, teach 'global before local skills' – the bigger picture of the expert routine prior to the required basic motor skills.

- 'Increasing complexity' – refine those gymnastic motor skills and enhance them.

- 'Increasing diversity' – perform those skills in a range of routines.

In furnishing the student with my thought processes, procedural heuristics and opportunities for reflection, they can make those gymnastic steps from apprentice to mastery, moving from the cognitive stage of learning towards autonomy in performance.

Dimension Four

SOCIOLOGY
Social characteristics of learning environments

The fourth and final dimension begins with ensuring the learning is 'situated', where students carry out tasks and solve problems in an environment that reflects the multiple uses to which their knowledge will be put in the future'. According to Collins et al., *situated learning* encourages students to actively use their knowledge, rather than just passively receive it, so they can see the purpose of their learning. They then encourage the development of *communities of practice* where students find an intrinsic motivation for their learning which goes beyond pleasing teachers or gaining examination grades, and where the students *exploit cooperation* between each other to enhance the community's learning as a whole.

SOCIOLOGY
Social characteristics of learning environments

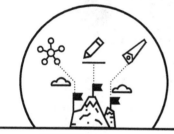

SITUATED LEARNING
Students learn in the context of
working on realistic tasks

COMMUNITY OF PRACTICE
Communication about different ways
to accomplish meaningful tasks

INTRINSIC MOTIVATION
Students set personal goals to
seek skills and solutions

COOPERATION
Students work together to
accomplish their goals

A summary introduction to Dimension Four: SOCIOLOGY

There is no step-by-step process to develop the *sociology* of cognitive apprenticeship as defined by Collins et al. In some ways, what they describe is creating a learning environment where students feel safe to share their ideas in an atmosphere where the work is genuinely valued by all those involved.

To be fair, I could have included all of the subject entries in the sociology section as without a safe classroom culture, little student thinking can ever be made visible. The three subjects I have chosen explicitly detail aspects of practice which meet with Collins et al.'s definition of 'sociology', cognitive apprenticeship's fourth dimension.

One of the aspects of learning art in Cassie Garbutt's lessons is the sense that teacher and students are 'all in it together'. Whilst what she describes is incredibly well structured, the visibility of the thinking in her lessons depends upon the students working as a community of learners, critiquing each other's work: 'In a safe environment, questions come at the student modeller in a constructive way. I will take back control for the next step of the portraiture process. Then a new student demonstrator steps up.'

In Beth Pelleymounter's drama lessons, there is a similar sense that teamwork is crucial to unpeeling the layers of thought: 'When creating theatre, we are constantly sharing our thinking processes, encouraging our students to develop their ideas through working *collaboratively*.' Beth's chapter details how to generate a collaborative ethos through the structures of cognitive apprenticeship.

We began this cognitive tour of academic subjects with biology, whose name derives from the Greek word *bios*, meaning 'life', and we end, fittingly, with an exploration of what that life means. When you are in Robin Parmiter's religion, philosophy and ethics classes, you feel as though you are engaged in the most important thinking you will ever encounter, something that offers you 'an improved ability to learn throughout life'.

Students love Robin's lessons because relationships in the class are healthy and the whole experience is built upon trust. Importantly, the learning is 'situated' in the truest sense. As Robin says, 'A key thinking process to share here (to engage all the students) is to understand that we are exploring *the meaning and purpose of our lives*, which is important for all of us!'

How on earth do you think like an artist? From Turner to Hirst, from Morisot to Emin, there are probably few common compositional thinking processes between them.

As Collins et al. point out, apprentice learners need 'continual access to models of expertise-in-use against which to refine their understanding of complex skills. Moreover, it is not uncommon for apprentices to have access to several masters and thus to a variety of models of expertise. Such richness and variety help them to understand that there may be multiple ways of carrying out a task and to recognize that no one individual embodies all knowledge or expertise.'

The trouble is, in an art classroom, we teach students the skills in a relatively subjective way. We show them the artistic output of different artists, but with one teacher in the classroom, we usually have one way of teaching the basic skills of composition.

I have been teaching art to secondary school students for nearly two decades. I have been a subject leader for over ten years now. I read a great deal about art practitioners. I love my subject.

My experience of how students learn has been hard earned. In my experience, the way we teach art can liberate or extinguish our students' distinctive creative impulses.

Students lose the creative freedoms they have if the classroom culture becomes too prescriptive. When we teach students the fundamental skills of observing and re-presenting, we have to teach students to have the disciplined *curiosity* to look and look again at what they are re-presenting in their art.

Once we teach them the skills and knowledge of artists, we need to give them the freedom to develop those skills according to how they see what they observe.

They need to understand the thinking processes of the expert artist during composition, to ensure they are reflective practitioners who are making deliberate decisions about the way they create, if they are going to become artists in their own right, with their unique style.

What we do when we teach students the skills of composition is to 'articulate the common aspects so that students can transfer what they learn' and thus develop their own distinct artistic skills.

Art teachers need to provide many opportunities for students to develop core artistic and visual skills, the formal elements. It is important to learn and practise these skills, to develop confidence in the skills, before questioning them, then experimenting with them, and finally unlearning them deliberately. Johnson-Laird articulated these sentiments precisely when he wrote, 'One cannot think creatively unless one has the knowledge with which to think creatively. Creativity represents a balance between knowledge and freeing oneself of that knowledge' (Johnson-Laird, 1988, cited in Sternberg, 2012).

To teach students the fundamental compositional skills they require whilst liberating them to put their own artistic stamp upon their work, I have developed the teacher-student-teacher-student demo. As Collins et al. point out, 'The teacher's thinking must be made visible to the students and the student's thinking must be made visible to the teacher.' In my model, we take that one step further, in that the student's thinking is made visible to the other students in the class.

Over six lessons, this is how the thinking processes of portraiture are made visible, following Collins et al.'s mantra that 'while each student practices soloing, the teacher as well as other students evaluate the soloist's performance'.

1. Teacher demo, where I complete a portrait, relentlessly verbalising the thinking processes behind my composition.

2. Teacher-student A-teacher-student B-teacher-student C demo, where I invite students to come up and we jointly compose a portrait, focusing on what they are observing and the decisions they make when they are composing.

3. Student D-student E-student F-student G-teacher-student H demo, where the students follow the same process as lesson 2 but I try very hard to remain quiet whilst students critique each other.

4. Individual student composition, with me coaching individuals to make their thinking visible.

5. Individual student composition, with me coaching individuals to make their thinking visible.

6. Hand-picked student L and student M present their work to the whole class, explaining the thinking processes behind their art and answering questions from their peers.

Within the structure of a project, such as drawing portraits, we all have our trusted method of how to sketch the shapes and mark out the proportions. We teach the students to draw these shapes accurately and with control, but we also want them to look, *really look*, to observe.

What struck me about the 'Cognitive Apprenticeship' paper was how it sharpened up my thoughts about modelling. As artists and art teachers, we spend a lot of time modelling. It is important when modelling to engage students in the task by explaining, at every step, what you are doing and why.

We are in the privileged position as the practising expert in the room. When students see us draw, paint and make, they do so with a sense of awe. But students can feel intimidated. An overly teacher-centric modelling session can stifle students' artistic endeavours, rather than stimulate them. I prefer the teacher-student-teacher-student-teacher-student demo. This is how the first lesson develops.

Let's stick with portraiture. Ensure that the materials you use are expendable. Begin with sketching out the dimensions of the face. Explain to the students what you are doing and why. Mimic the questions that are going on in your head, about what you are drawing, what you are thinking, what you are observing.

I find it important to rehearse the articulation of my thinking processes. Practising the articulation of your thinking is crucial if you are to become an expert modeller.

A quick switch from teacher demo to student demo is crucial if you are to prevent it becoming an intimidating teacher-expert event. Model with prompts for next steps: *What would you do? Here you go, carry on for me.* Hand over the brush/charcoal/pencil.

Students then take over. It is illuminating. In a safe environment, questions come at the student modeller in a constructive way. I will take back control for the next step of the portraiture process. Then a new student demonstrator steps up.

I have not only articulated my thought processes for the students but also modelled how to articulate my thought processes in a specific way:

> At the beginning, I always ask myself, 'What about this man's face is his distinctive feature? What is it that I want to emphasise, spend as much

time on as possible to get right?' Once I know that – and it often comes immediately, but other times I have to observe even harder than normal – I work on the portrait with that feature in mind all the time. Then I start with the dimensions. This is key. One thing I always check is whether I have the cheek bones in the right place, relative to the nose. That is crucial to getting the facial dimensions accurate.

Metacognitively standing outside myself and talking about myself in the third person emphasises the decision-making processes much more explicitly.

Students begin with knowledge of artists and their techniques. They arrive at the end of the six lessons with heuristic processes for representing every aspect of portraiture, having made those heuristics their own by using metacognitive thinking processes which they have learnt from listening and watching their teacher and their peers.

The teacher-peer modelling prevents just the teacher's subjective artistic techniques influencing the students. There is genuine dialogue as the expert and the apprentices learn through making their thinking visible.

MAKING THINKING VISIBLE IN...
DRAMA
BY BETH PELLEYMOUNTER

How to become an expert thinker when **creating theatre** is the linchpin to incorporating the vast range of skills that our drama students are required to learn and develop.

How do we teach such an important expert thinking process? **Modelling** is vitally important at the beginning of this journey; as Collins et al. suggest, observation has a key role to play in students' learning. Students need the opportunity to experience many genres of theatre and powerful devising work, whether digitally or in person, professional or by other students. I often show them an occasional performance of my own. If I am asking them to perform and be vulnerable, then so will I. This provides an opportunity to share with less confident students how this makes me feel and offer heuristic strategies to overcome nerves. It is important to establish honest discussion about the analysis of what they have seen. Drawing key questions: 'What worked? What did not? What elements of this could you use in your own work? What element of the work affected you and why?' Students therefore see modelling through discussion, analysis and dissection of what is effective theatre, a framework of what to aim for.

Once the students have a vision of *what* they could create, I then move into the process of *how* to do it. **Scaffolding** is an important tool in this stage. I show them an insight into how my mind would work when needing to develop key elements of the stimulus and mould them into a scene for the piece. In one lesson we explored how to use choral work to present transitional scenes, while using the historical arguments for and against women having the vote, having used the Suffragettes as stimulus. I have delivered workshops that introduce Frantic Assembly's 'chair duet' sequences and scaffold how to adapt this technique while using the excerpt of Emmeline Pankhurst's account of force feeding. This breaks down the process into clear, easy-to-follow steps and uses modelling throughout so that students can see examples of what they are aiming for. During this process, we watch each other's works in progress, revisiting the analysis phase to help improve and develop each time. In A level work, I would pull out key characteristics of their chosen practitioner and deliver workshops on each of these. For example, when working in the style of the Kneehigh theatre company, I provide a tick list of rules to follow when working with puppets and embedding these into their scenes. This practical scaffolding can provide students with a simple springboard to help them devise their own scenes, or for those students needing more support, a template to stick more closely to.

In addition to these structured workshops, it is important to instil the importance not only of creativity but also of organisation. In order to do this, there is transparency about key dates and deadlines that they need to meet in order to have their pieces ready. I will ask them to create and complete rehearsal schedules, scaffold how I would complete mine and prompt them to continually review and amend their plans when needed – all transferable skills for other subjects.

It is at this stage that I would become a **coach**, giving the students the freedom to create, take ownership of their work, and let their piece breathe and grow. As a coach, I will always be watching, listening, observing and checking they are on track. When the moment presents itself, I ask questions, challenging them, encouraging them to reflect. It is when a scene goes wrong that the learning curve can be at its greatest, but with support they can find a solution. It is during this time that I feel it is important that students see clearly that as teachers we do not have all of the answers and that we are on this organic journey alongside them, finding the answer through discussion and exploration. If I don't know about the subject area that they are devising, I will ensure I learn alongside them, modelling that learning is lifelong. The ensuing conversations with my students – such as 'Emily, I was thinking about your work last night. What do you think about this idea…?' or 'Ben, I was reading that book you mentioned. I am interested as to why you chose that character?' – are so powerful.

In the **fading** aspect of cognitive apprenticeship, I encourage the students to interchange who takes on the role of the 'teacher'. Students then delegate areas of research that need to be completed, taking it in turns to be 'teacher' and share their findings in their next lesson. I often give them the task to develop an idea for a scene based on their findings, a process that helps the students develop their independence and leadership skills. Relationships are important throughout, developing and establishing a learning environment of respect and trust, encouraging students to analyse others' work through articulation by both teacher and student.

Collins et al.'s 'Cognitive Apprenticeship' approach is at the core of the devising process, where 'teaching methods are designed to give students the opportunity to observe, engage in, and invent or discover expert strategies'.

I find it encouraging that when creating theatre, we are constantly sharing our thinking processes, encouraging our students to develop their ideas through work collaboratively. Collin's et al. refer to 'articulation', 'reflection' and 'exploration', all of which can be constantly developed when problem-solving and moving a piece forward through the discussions that teacher and students have throughout the creative process that is devising.

Without using the cognitive apprenticeship model, I find that devised pieces are often predictable and simplistic in terms of drama techniques. I will always remember with pride a GCSE group who created a piece of theatre based on the *Titanic*. They were a group with a wide range of skills. From the beginning, they were engaged and excited about the stimulus due to the hook that launched the project. The students entered the lesson in darkness with the sound of sirens, the sea and a string quartet. Throughout the process, they worked as a group to take it in turns to take on the role of the teacher and expert to pass on the knowledge that they had researched and to direct each other in their idea for a scene. All the while they used the scaffolded ideas that I had practically explored with them at the beginning of the project. They responded well to teacher prompts to keep a close eye on their well-planned-out rehearsal schedule and articulated objectives.

The devising journey was not always smooth – it never is! But with the disagreements that the students had or blanks that they reached with the creation of scenes, I observed and, when needed, coached them through asking them pertinent questions. The factor that worked so well was the transparency within the group. We were all on this journey together. We had open discussions about their creative thoughts and mine, developing a heuristic approach to learning.

As suggested, it is up to the individual teacher to develop these four main aspects of cognitive apprenticeship within their own pedagogy in order to help students develop and master skills that are not subject specific but transferable, creating a heuristic approach to learning. I believe that, throughout the drama curriculum, time and time again this model provides students with a framework on which to base their learning and thereby increase their skills and knowledge.

RELIGION, PHILOSOPHY AND ETHICS

BY ROBIN PARMITER

In religion, philosophy and ethics, we deliberately and explicitly bring expert thinking to the surface. We have to. All we mostly do is think! And we create a community where, as Collins et al. explain, we design activities 'to engender a community of practice for reading' where 'students and teacher [discuss] how they interpret what they read'. The following processes are used in a variety of tasks, helping students plan, monitor and evaluate their written and verbal arguments. At their heart, they embed in students' brains disciplinary thinking processes which prepare them to live a life worth living.

Religion and theology

How to reach judgements on which religious beliefs and practices are most important and valid for a particular religious community?

One of the most common thinking errors our students make when evaluating religious beliefs is to state 'I'm not religious' or 'I'm an atheist', etc. That's great. But it's not relevant to the particular 'game' we're playing. Different games have different rules, I explain. Many students have never played 'Christian theology' or 'Buddhism' before. Students from within religious communities often have an advantage here. They get that these questions are important for certain people *within* communities.

A key thinking process to share here (to engage all the students) is to understand that we are exploring *the meaning and purpose of our lives!* Which is important for all of us. The answers will guide our decisions, feelings and actions. Whether we know it or not, we all have a 'religion' in one sense – a belief system and metanarrative that guides us. A religion is essentially a more formalised and institutionalised answer to resolving the ultimate question of the meaning of life. In order to explore, understand and evaluate these 'answers', we need to think from *within* them. We need to understand the rules of the game. We need to speak the language.

Therefore, a key process is to make visible *how to think inside the world of the particular religion* we're studying. What I have shaped over years of teaching

RPE is a Collins et al.-style thought-heuristic which is based on a number of artfully crafted questions.

To begin with, I ask the following: 'What is the language of this world? What are the symbols and stories? What are the rules? What are sources of authority?' And in order to make a value judgement, we must have some kind of success criteria; within religion, this is measured according to the fulfilment of an *ultimate purpose*. Therefore, the key question that needs to be made visible before making a judgement about specific religious beliefs and practices is 'What is the *ultimate purpose* of this religion?' Usually, there isn't just one answer. Within a particular religion there are multiple views. So the next part of my thinking is to ask, 'What are the different views?' And in order to answer this question, we must also ask, 'What do the sources of authority say? Are there different ways of interpreting these teachings? Which source has more authority, and why?'

For example, within Christianity, although it could be claimed that the *ultimate purpose* is 'salvation', this could be defined in terms of 'going to heaven' or 'bringing heaven to earth' or 'a bit of both' (it could also be argued that salvation is not the aim at all). My value judgement of the particular belief or practice will depend on the specific view of salvation or *ultimate purpose*. Just being aware of this (and making it visible) is part of being an expert.

The next part of the process is to ask how people from within this religion achieve this *ultimate purpose*. Again, there are different views. 'What are the various views?' And in order to answer this question, we must again ask 'What do the sources of authority say? Are there different ways of interpreting these teachings? Which source has more authority, and why?'

The answer to these questions will influence the final judgement (*not* The Final Judgement – although, who knows, perhaps it will!). Ultimately, it is the process of asking these questions, exploring a multiplicity of possible answers and interpretations, that makes someone an expert thinker on religion.

Philosophy for life

How to analyse beliefs?

A thinking-heuristic is central to analysing beliefs and I have outlined our thinking-heuristic process here.

According to Socrates, 'the unexamined life is not worth living'. This is the claim at the heart of our 'Philosophy for Life' course. And it is true simply because if we don't examine the beliefs, values and opinions we have absorbed from our family, culture and religion, we cannot really claim that our life is actually *ours*. But how on earth do we test a belief? Socrates argued that, just as a potter develops a method to ensure their pots are watertight, we must develop a process to test whether our beliefs really hold up to the light of reason. Why? Because ignorance is not bliss. Our beliefs will ultimately guide our emotional reactions, behaviours and choices. Consequently, at Huntington we make visible a Socratic method of thinking and questioning.

The first process is to identify the belief (either a commonly held view, a personal opinion or an unspoken and assumed belief that is underpinning an action). 'What is the belief?' This might sound obvious, but it is amazing how often our beliefs aren't even recognized as beliefs – so much is assumed to be true (beliefs often remain unconscious and unexamined) e.g. the belief that *the point of life is to be happy*; or *life should be fair*; or *it's good to be yourself*; or *it's good to be monogamous*; or *only scientific knowledge is true knowledge*; or *a good job is a well-paid job* etc.

The second process is to find an exception: 'Can any exceptions be found?' Let's take the belief '*a good job is a well-paid job*'. Can an exception be found? Yes, a job isn't good if it's well-paid yet completely unfulfilling.

The third process is to conclude that **if an exception can be found, then it must not be completely true.**

The next process is to **modify the original belief to incorporate the exception:** '*a good job is a well-paid and fulfilling job*'.

The next process is to again find an exception: 'Can any exceptions be found?' Yes, a job isn't good if it is both well-paid and fulfilling yet causes lots of harm to others.

The expert thinker can repeat this process of modifying beliefs and finding exceptions. And the belief that can't finally be disproved (that is to say, a belief free from exceptions) is a true belief. No wonder Socrates concluded: '*One thing only I know, and that is that I know nothing.*' And he was declared by the Oracle at Delphi to be the wisest person in Athens!

And philosophy, after all, is 'the love of wisdom'. To be Socratic is to be expert. **Or is it? Can any exceptions be found? Yes...(Here we go again!)**

Ethics and philosophy of religion

How to analyse arguments and theories?

The first, fundamental, process is to ask, 'What is the idea/concept/scholar arguing?' i.e. 'What are they claiming? Am I right in my understanding? Have

I understood this correctly?' It's amazing how many students want to skip this foundational stage; they would much rather dive into playful discussion and pontification (of course there is a place for that – we use thought experiments and big questions to structure these).

The next process is to ask, 'What is persuasive about this idea/concept/scholar? What are the positive implications? What is the supporting evidence, reason and rationality?'

The next process is to ask, 'What is problematic about this idea/concept/ scholar? What are the negative implications? Does the argument actually work? Or does it commit a fallacy or two?'

The next process is to ask how far the positives outweigh the negatives, or vice versa. 'Which side wins? Why?' (It could be to do with the quantity of the objections or the quality of one defence.)

The next process is to **identify and repeat for each relevant idea/concept/ scholar within the argument or theory.**

And finally, weigh up all the points against each other to reach a conclusion: Overall, 'How far is this argument/theory persuasive? Based on all the reasons, counterpoints, problems and strengths, what can I convincingly conclude? Does my conclusion match up to all the thinking that preceded it?'

The expert thinker examines and evaluates each aspect of an argument or theory. They are both defence and prosecution, judge and jury. The expert thinker facilitates a fair and thorough trial.

So, Collins et al. are spot on. In my subject, religion, philosophy and ethics, making thinking visible is at the very core of my working day. The thinking processes I have outlined here have been practised by me for years upon literally thousands of willing students. Practising these questions yourself as a teacher will help embed them in your teaching brain. It is the first step in helping your students to become expert thinkers on religion, philosophy and ethics and for them to acquire 'an improved ability to learn throughout life'.

CONCLUSION

Now that you have read *Cognitive Apprenticeship In Action*, I hope you are keen to debate how you make expert disciplinary thinking in your subject visible, both with my colleagues at Huntington and, more importantly, with your own colleagues at your school. As I wrote in my introduction, *informed debate is the fuel of curriculum development.*

When we set out to write this book, I asked my colleagues three fundamental questions:

1. How do you think like an expert (very specifically) in your subject discipline?

2. How do you make that expert subject disciplinary thinking visible to students?

3. How do you teach your students to be expert subject disciplinary thinkers?

Now, you will have realised that to begin answering question 1, you have to identify what, exactly, is the core substantive knowledge in your discipline. And that is an endless discussion. My colleagues' responses were inherently subjective and partial. But the debate is key. A healthy department in a healthy school will be debating curriculum issues regularly and frequently – what to include within your subject offer to students and what to leave out.

In order to complete an answer to question 1, you need to go beyond the substantive and consider your subject's disciplinary knowledge, which Christine Counsell (2018) defined beautifully thus: 'Disciplinary knowledge is a curricular term for what pupils learn about how that knowledge was established, its degree of certainty, and how it continues to be revised by scholars, artists or professional practice. It is that part of the subject where pupils understand each discipline as a tradition of enquiry with its own distinctive pursuit of truth.' In other words, disciplinary knowledge is the way subject experts debate their subject to come to a profound understanding of the essence of history or science or English literature or any of the subjects studied in our schools.

Once you have established your subject's core substantive and disciplinary knowledge, you then have to make the thinking required to establish that substantive and disciplinary knowledge visible to your students, which is the essence of question 2.

And then, finally, an answer to question 3 will identify the cognitive apprenticeship techniques required to make visible to your students the thought processes needed to apply substantive and disciplinary knowledge to solve problems or answer questions in your respective subject discipline.

None of what I have written above is an attempt to make things more complicated than necessary. But thinking hard about your subject discipline is intellectually challenging. Many teachers I know were originally inspired to teach by their subject, and debating the subjects they love needs to be privileged in schools. Providing the time for colleagues to engage in such conversations makes the job of being a teacher in our country's schools more attractive.

Teaching your students to think like a subject expert is at the heart of cognitive apprenticeship. Making your expert thinking visible is key, once you have agreed as a subject team exactly what constitutes expert thinking in your subject. If you consider our three questions again, they make up a clear three-stage process for you and your colleagues to work through:

1. How do you think like an expert (very specifically) in your subject discipline? (**Think through and collectively agree your expert substantive and disciplinary knowledge.**)

2. How do you make that expert subject disciplinary thinking visible to students? (**Decide how to articulate your expert thinking to your students.**)

3. How do you teach your students to be expert subject disciplinary thinkers? (**Decide how to teach your students to think like a subject expert using the four dimensions of cognitive apprenticeship.**)

The four dimensions of cognitive apprenticeship will sound familiar to many of you who have read this book. It would be easy to conclude that you are already using cognitive apprenticeship techniques in your classroom. But that is not really the point. I will finish provocatively with a fourth question for you to answer, and that goes something like this: 'How *faithfully* are you using the four dimensions of cognitive apprenticeship in your teaching?' If you tackle that question along with the other three I have explored above, you'll have fuel aplenty to drive curriculum development in your subject, and make disciplinary thinking visible to the benefit of your students.

BIBLIOGRAPHY

Brown, J. S., Collins, A. and Duguid, P. (1989) 'Situated cognition and the culture of learning', *Educational Researcher* 18 (1) pp. 32–42.

Caviglioli, O. (2019) *Dual coding with teachers*. Woodbridge: John Catt Educational.

Christodoulou, D. (2017) *Making good progress?* Oxford: OUP.

Collins, A., Brown, J. S. and Holum, A. (1991) 'Cognitive apprenticeship: making thinking visible', *American Educator* 15 (4) pp. 6–11, 38–46.

Collins, A., Brown, J. S. and Newman, S. E. (1989) 'Cognitive apprenticeship: teaching the craft of reading, writing and mathematics' in Resnick, L. B. (ed.) *Knowing, learning, and instruction: essays in honor of Robert Glaser*. Hillsdale, NJ: Lawrence Erlbaum.

Counsell, C. (2018) 'Taking curriculum seriously', *Impact* 4. Retrieved from: www.bit.ly/38MXnZJ

Department for Education (2013) *National curriculum in England: computing programmes of study*. London: The Stationery Office. Retrieved from: www.bit.ly/3o56Rra

EEF (2018) 'Mastery learning', *Teaching & learning toolkit* [Online]. London: EEF. Retrieved from: www.bit.ly/39S2qKY

Flavell, J. (1976) 'Metacognitive aspects of problem-solving' in Resnick, L. (ed.) *The nature of intelligence*. Hillsdale, NJ: Lawrence Erlbaum, pp. 231–236.

Graham, S., Bruch, J., Fitzgerald, J., Friedrich, L., Furgeson, J., Greene, K., Kim, J., Lyskawa, J., Olson, C. B. and Smither Wulsin, C. (2016) *Teaching secondary students to write effectively*. Washington, DC: National Center for Education Evaluation and Regional Assistance (NCEE), Institute of Education Sciences, US Department of Education.

Holman, J. and Yeomans, E. (2018) *Improving secondary science*. London: EEF.

Laffin, D. (2013) 'Marr: magpie or marsh harrier?', *Teaching History* 149 (1) pp. 18–25. Retrieved from: www.bit.ly/3neX4PH

Muijs, D. and Bokhove, C. (2020) *Metacognition and self-regulation: evidence review.* London: EEF. Retrieved from: www.bit.ly/3qFNEP2

OCR (2020) *Coding challenges booklet: coding challenges for both GCSE and A level.* Cambridge: OCR. Retrieved from: www.bit.ly/2NkW8Mv

O'Hare, L., Stark, P., Cockerill, M., Lloyd, K., McConnellogue, S., Gildea, A., Biggart, A., Connolly, P. and Bower, C. (2019) *Reciprocal reading: evaluation report.* London: EEF. Retrieved from: www.bit.ly/2MW8yu2

Palincsar, A. S. and Brown, A. L. (1984) 'Reciprocal teaching of comprehension-fostering and monitoring activities', *Cognition and Instruction* 1 (2) pp. 117–175.

Quigley, A. and Coleman, R. (2019) *Improving literacy in secondary schools.* London: EEF.

Quigley, A., Muijs, D. and Stringer, E. (2018) *Metacognition and self-regulated learning.* London: EEF. Retrieved from: www.bit.ly/2YZvdqE

Rosenshine, B. (2012) 'Principles of instruction: research-based strategies that all teachers should know', *American Educator* 36 (1) pp. 12–19, 39. Retrieved from: www.bit.ly/2Kw17qg

Salters' Institute (2018) 'Best evidence science teaching', *STEM Learning* [Website]. Retrieved from: www.bit.ly/3bvafZF

Scardamalia, M. and Bereiter, C. (1983) 'The development of evaluative, diagnostic and remedial capabilities in children's composing' in Martlew, M. (ed.) *The psychology of written language: a developmental approach.* London: Wiley, pp. 67–95.

Scardamalia. M. and Bereiter, C. (1985) 'Fostering the development of self-regulation in children's knowledge processing' in Chipman, S. F., Segal, J. W. and Glaser, R. (eds) *Thinking and learning skills: research and open questions.* Hillsdale, NJ: Lawrence Erlbaum, pp. 563–577.

Scardamalia, M., Bereiter, C. and Steinbach, R. (1984) 'Teachability of reflective process in written composition', *Cognitive Science* 8 (2) pp. 173–190.

Schmitt, N., Jiang, X. and Grabe, W. (2011) 'The percentage of words known in a text and reading comprehension', *The Modern Language Journal* 95 (1) pp. 26–43.

Schoenfeld, A. H. (1983) *Problem-solving in the mathematics curriculum.* Washington, DC: The Mathematical Association of America.

Schoenfeld, A. H. (1985) *Mathematical problem-solving.* New York, NY: Academic Press.

Sherrington, T. (2019) *Rosenshine's principles in action.* Woodbridge: John Catt Educational.

Sternberg, R. J. (2012) 'The assessment of creativity: an investment-based approach', *Creativity Research Journal* 24 (1) pp. 3–12.

Sweller, J., van Merrienboer, J. J. G. and Paas, F. G. W. C. (1998) 'Cognitive architecture and instructional design', *Educational Psychology Review* 10 (1) pp. 251–296.

Sweller, J. (2006) 'The worked example effect and human cognition', *Learning and Instruction* 16 (2) pp. 165–169.

Tomsett, J. and Uttley, J. (2020) *Putting staff first.* Woodbridge: John Catt Educational.

'COGNITIVE APPRENTICESHIP: MAKING THINKING VISIBLE' (1991)

BY ALLAN COLLINS, JOHN SEELY BROWN AND ANN HOLUM

Reprinted with permission from the Winter 1991 issue of *American Educator*, the quarterly journal of the American Federation of Teachers, American Federation of Labor and Congress of Industrial Organizations.

In ancient times, teaching and learning were accomplished through apprenticeship: we taught our children how to speak, grow crops, craft cabinets, or tailor clothes by showing them how and by helping them do it. Apprenticeship was the vehicle for transmitting the knowledge required for expert practice in fields from painting and sculpting to medicine and law. It was the natural way to learn. In modern times, apprenticeship has largely been replaced by formal schooling, except in children's learning of language, in some aspects of graduate education, and in on-the-job training. We propose an alternative model of instruction that is accessible within the framework of the typical American classroom. It is a model of instruction that goes back to apprenticeship but incorporates elements of schooling. We call this model 'cognitive apprenticeship' (Collins, Brown, and Newman, 1989).

While there are many differences between schooling and apprenticeship methods, we will focus on one. In apprenticeship, learners can see the processes of work: they watch a parent sow, plant, and harvest crops and help as they are able; they assist a tradesman as he crafts a cabinet; they piece together garments under the supervision of a more experienced tailor. Apprenticeship involves learning a physical, tangible activity. But in schooling, the 'practice' of problem-solving, reading comprehension, and writing is not at all obvious – it is not necessarily observable to the student. In apprenticeship, the processes of the activity are visible. In schooling, the processes of thinking are often invisible to both the students and the teacher. Cognitive apprenticeship is a model of instruction that works to make thinking visible.

In this article, we will present some of the features of traditional apprenticeship and discuss the ways it can be adapted to the teaching and learning of cognitive skills. Then we will present three successful examples – cases in which teachers and researchers have used apprenticeship methods to teach reading, writing, and mathematics.

In the final section, we organize our ideas about the characteristics of successful teaching into a general framework for the design of learning environments, where 'environment' includes the content taught, the pedagogical methods employed, the sequencing of learning activities, and the sociology of learning.

TOWARD A SYNTHESIS OF SCHOOLING AND APPRENTICESHIP

Although schools have been relatively successful in organizing and conveying large bodies of conceptual and factual knowledge, standard pedagogical practices render key aspects of expertise invisible to students. Too little attention is paid to the reasoning and strategies that experts employ when they acquire knowledge or put it to work to solve complex or real-life tasks. Where such processes are addressed, the emphasis is on formulaic methods for solving 'textbook' problems or on the development of low-level subskills in relative isolation.

As a result, conceptual and problem-solving knowledge acquired in school remains largely inert for many students. In some cases, knowledge remains bound to surface features of problems as they appear in textbooks and class presentations. For example, Schoenfeld (1985) has found that, in solving mathematics problems, students rely on their knowledge of standard textbook patterns of problem presentation rather than on their knowledge of problem-solving strategies or intrinsic properties of the problems themselves. When they encounter problems that fall outside these patterns, students are often at a loss for what to do. In other cases, students fail to use resources available to them to improve their skills because they lack models of how to tap into those resources. For example, students are unable to make use of potential models of good writing acquired through reading because they have no understanding of how the authors produced such text. Stuck with what Scardamalia and Bereiter (1985) call 'knowledge-telling strategies,' they are unaware that expert writing involves organizing one's ideas about a topic, elaborating goals to be achieved in the writing, thinking about what the audience is likely to know or believe about the subject, and so on.

To make real differences in students' skill, we need both to understand the nature of expert practice and to devise methods that are appropriate to learning that practice. To do this, we must first recognize that cognitive strategies are central to integrating skills and knowledge in order to accomplish meaningful tasks. They are the organizing principles of expertise, particularly in such domains as reading, writing, and mathematics. Further, because expert practice in these domains rests crucially on the integration of cognitive strategies, we believe that it can best be taught through methods that have traditionally been employed in apprenticeship to transmit complex physical processes and skills.

Traditional Apprenticeship

In traditional apprenticeship, the expert shows the apprentice how to do a task, watches as the apprentice practices portions of the task, and then turns over more and more responsibility until the apprentice is proficient enough to accomplish the task independently. That is the basic notion of apprenticeship: showing the apprentice how to do a task and helping the apprentice to do it. There are four important aspects of traditional apprenticeship: modelling, scaffolding, fading, and coaching.

In modelling, the apprentice observes the master demonstrating how to do different parts of the task. The master makes the target processes visible, often by explicitly showing the apprentice what to do. But as Lave and Wenger (1991) point out, in traditional apprenticeship, much of the learning occurs as apprentices watch others at work.

Scaffolding is the support the master gives apprentices in carrying out a task. This can range from doing almost the entire task for them to giving occasional hints as to what to do next. Fading is the notion of slowly removing the support, giving the apprentice more and more responsibility.

Coaching is the thread running through the entire apprenticeship experience. The master coaches the apprentice through a wide range of activities: choosing tasks, providing hints and scaffolding, evaluating the activities of apprentices and diagnosing the kinds of problems they are having, challenging them and offering encouragement, giving feedback, structuring the ways to do things, working on particular weaknesses. In short, coaching is the process of overseeing the student's learning.

The interplay among observation, scaffolding, and increasingly independent practice aids apprentices both in developing self-monitoring and correction skills and in integrating the skills and conceptual knowledge needed to advance toward expertise. Observation plays a surprisingly key role; Lave

(1988) hypothesizes that it aids learners in developing a conceptual model of the target task prior to attempting to execute it. Giving students a conceptual model-a picture of the whole-is an important factor in apprenticeship's success in teaching complex skills without resorting to lengthy practice of isolated subskills, for three related reasons. First, it provides learners with an advanced organizer for their initial attempts to execute a complex skill, thus allowing them to concentrate more of their attention on execution than would otherwise be possible. Second, a conceptual model provides an interpretive structure for making sense of the feedback, hints, and corrections from the master during interactive coaching sessions. Third, it provides an internalized guide for the period when the apprentice is engaged in relatively independent practice.

Another key observation about apprenticeship concerns the social context in which learning takes place. Apprenticeship derives many cognitively important characteristics from being embedded in a subculture in which most, if not all, members are participants in the target skills. As a result, learners have continual access to models of expertise-in-use against which to refine their understanding of complex skills. Moreover, it is not uncommon for apprentices to have access to several masters and thus to a variety of models of expertise. Such richness and variety help them to understand that there may be multiple ways of carrying out a task and to recognize that no one individual embodies all knowledge or expertise. And finally, learners have the opportunity to observe other learners with varying degrees of skill; among other things, this encourages them to view learning as an incrementally staged process, while providing them with concrete benchmarks for their own progress.

From Traditional to Cognitive Apprenticeship

There are three important differences between traditional apprenticeship and the kind of cognitive apprenticeship we propose.

As we said, in traditional apprenticeship, the process of carrying out a task to be learned is usually easily observable. In cognitive apprenticeship, one needs to deliberately bring the thinking to the surface, to make it visible, whether it's in reading, writing, problem-solving. The teacher's thinking must be made visible to the students and the student's thinking must be made visible to the teacher. That is the most important difference between traditional apprenticeship and cognitive apprenticeship. Cognitive research, through such methods as protocol analysis, has begun to delineate the cognitive and metacognitive processes that comprise expertise. By bringing these tacit processes into the open, students can observe, enact, and practice them with help from the teacher and from other students.

Second, in traditional apprenticeship, the tasks come up just as they arise in the world: learning is completely situated in the workplace. When tasks arise in the context of designing and creating tangible products, apprentices naturally understand the reasons for undertaking the process of apprenticeship. They are motivated to work and to learn the subcomponents of the task, because they realize the value of the finished product. They retain what they must do to complete the task, because they have seen the expert's model of the finished product, and so the subcomponents of the task make sense. But in school, teachers are working with a curriculum centered around reading, writing, science, math, history, etc. that is, in large part, divorced from what students and most adults do in their lives. In cognitive apprenticeship, then, the challenge is to situate the abstract tasks of the school curriculum in contexts that make sense to students.

Third, in traditional apprenticeship, the skills to be learned inhere in the task itself: to craft a garment, the apprentice learns some skills unique to tailoring, for example, stitching buttonholes. Cabinetry does not require that the apprentice know anything about buttonholes. In other words, in traditional apprenticeship, it is unlikely that students encounter situations in which the transfer of skills is required. The tasks in schooling, however, demand that students be able to transfer what they learn. In cognitive apprenticeship, the challenge is to present a range of tasks, varying from systematic to diverse, and to encourage students to reflect on and articulate the elements that are common across tasks. As teachers present the targeted skills to students, they can increasingly vary the contexts in which those skills are useful. The goal is to help students generalize the skill, to learn when the skill is or is not applicable, and to transfer the skill independently when faced with novel situations.

In order to translate the model of traditional apprenticeship to cognitive apprenticeship, teachers need to:

- identify the processes of the task and make them visible to students;

- situate abstract tasks in authentic contexts, so that students understand the relevance of the work; and

- vary the diversity of situations and articulate the common aspects so that students can transfer what they learn.

We do not want to argue that cognitive apprenticeship is the only way to learn. Reading a book or listening to a lecture are important ways to learn, particularly in domains where conceptual and factual knowledge are central. Active listeners or readers, who test their understanding and pursue the issues that are raised in their minds, learn things that apprenticeship can never teach. To the degree that readers or listeners are passive, however, they will not learn as much as they would by apprenticeship, because apprenticeship forces them to use their knowledge. Moreover, few people learn to be active readers and listeners on their own, and that is where cognitive apprenticeship is critical-observing the processes by which an expert listener or reader thinks and practicing these skills under the guidance of the expert can teach students to learn on their own more skilfully.

Even in domains that rest on elaborate conceptual and factual underpinnings, students must learn the practice or art of solving problems and carrying out tasks. And to achieve expert practice, some version of apprenticeship remains the method of choice.

COGNITIVE APPRENTICESHIP TEACHING READING WRITING AND MATHEMATICS

In this section, we will briefly describe three success models of teaching in the foundational domains of reading, writing, and mathematics and how these models embody the basic methods of cognitive apprenticeship. These three domains are foundational not only because they provide the basis for learning and communication in other school subjects but also because they engage cognitive and metacognitive processes that are basic to learning and thinking more generally. Unlike school subjects such as chemistry or history, these domains rest on relatively sparse conceptual and factual underpinnings, turning instead on students' robust and efficient execution of a set of cognitive and metacognitive skills. As such, we believe they are particularly well suited to teaching methods modeled on cognitive apprenticeship.

Reading

Palincsar and Brown's (1984) *reciprocal teaching* of reading exemplifies many of the features of cognitive apprenticeship. It has proved remarkably effective in raising students' scores on reading comprehension tests, especially those of poor readers. The basic method centers on modeling and coaching students in four strategic skills: formulating questions based on the text, summarizing the text, making predictions about what will come next, and clarifying difficulties with the text. Reciprocal teaching was originally designed for middle school students who could decode adequately but had serious comprehension problems; it can be adapted to any age group. The method has been used with groups of two to seven students, as well as individual students. It is called reciprocal teaching because the teacher and students take turns playing the role of teacher.

The procedure is as follows: both the teacher and students read a paragraph silently. Whoever is playing the role of teacher formulates a question based on the paragraph, constructs a summary, and makes a prediction or clarification, if any come to mind. Initially, the teacher models this process and then turns the role of teacher over to the students. When students first undertake the process, the teacher coaches them extensively on how to construct good questions and summaries, offering prompts and critiquing their efforts. In this way, the teacher provides scaffolding for the students, enabling them to take on whatever portion of the task they are able to. As the students become more proficient, the teacher fades, assuming the role of monitor and providing occasional hints or feedback. The transcript below shows the kind of scaffolding and group interaction that occurs with children during reciprocal teaching.

SAMPLE RECIPROCAL TEACHING DIALOGUE
(from Palincsar, 1986)

Text from which students are working

Crows have another gift. They are great mimics. They can learn to talk and imitate animal sounds. Some have been known to learn 100 words and even whole phrases. They can imitate the squawk of a chicken, the whine of a dog, or the meow of a cat.

Games have a certain fascination to crows. In a game of hide and seek, a crow hides in the hollow of a tree and then sounds a distress caw. The others rush to the spot, look around, then flap away. This may be done over and over, after which the young crow pops out of its hiding place and caws gleefully. Far from being annoyed at this, the flock bursts into loud cawing themselves. They seem to like the trick that has been played on them.

T:	Chantel, you're our teacher, right? Why don't you summarize first? Remember, just tell me the most important parts.
S1:	Crows have a hundred words they can learn by imitation. They can imitate chickens, the whine of a dog, and cats.
T:	Okay. We can shorten that summary a bit.
S2:	You could say they can imitate other animals.
T:	Oh! Good one! There's a list there, Chantel, did you notice that? It says they can imitate the squawk of a chicken, the whine of a dog or the meow of a cat; and you could call that 'animal sounds.' Can you ask us a question?
S1:	Ain't no questions in here.

S3:	The words [sic] that need to be clarified are [sic] 'mimics.'
S4:	That means imitate, right?
T:	Right. How did you figure that out, Shirley?
S4:	The paragraph.
T:	Show us how somebody could figure out what 'mimic' means.
S5:	They are great mimics. They can learn to talk and imitate animal sounds.
T:	Yes, so the next sentence tells you what it means. Very good, anything else needs to be clarified?
All:	No.
T:	What about that question we need to ask? (pause) What is the second paragraph about, Chantel?
S1:	The games they play.
S3:	They do things like people do.
S4:	What kinds of games do crows play?
S3:	Hide and seek. Over and over again.
T:	You know what, Larry? That was a real good comparison. One excellent question could be, 'How are crows like people?'
S4:	They play hide and seek.
T:	Good. Any other questions there?
S2:	How come the crows don't get annoyed?
S5:	Because they like it, they have fun. If I had a crow, I'd tell him he was it and see what he'd do.
T:	Let's summarize now and have some predictions.
S1:	This was about how they play around in games.
T:	Good for you. That's it. Predictions anyone?
S2:	Maybe more tricks they play.
S4:	Other games.
T:	Maybe. So far, they have told us several ways that crows are very smart; they can communicate with one another, they can imitate many sounds, and they play games. Maybe we will read about another way in which they are smart. Who will be the next teacher?

Reciprocal teaching is extremely effective. In a pilot study with individual students who were poor readers, the method raised their reading comprehension test scores from 15 percent to 85 percent accuracy after about twenty training sessions. Six months later the students were still at 60 percent accuracy; recovering to 85 percent only after one session. In a subsequent study with groups of two students, the scores increased dorm about 30 percent to 80 percent accuracy, with very little change eight weeks later. In classroom studies of groups of four to seven students, test scores increased from about 40 percent to 80 percent correct, again with only a slight decline eight weeks later. These are very dramatic effects for any instructional intervention.

Why is reciprocal teaching so effective? In our analysis, which reflects in part the views of Palincsar and Brown, its effectiveness depends upon the co concurrence of a number of factors.

First, the method engages students in a set of activities that help them form a new conceptual model of the task of reading. In traditional schooling, students learn to identify reading with the subskills of recognizing and pronouncing words and with the activities of scanning text and saying it aloud. Under the new conception, students recognize that reading requires constructive activities, such as formulating questions and making summaries and predictions, as well as evaluative ones, such as analyzing and clarifying the pints of difficulty. As Palincsar points out (1987), working with a text in a discussion format is not the same as teaching isolated comprehension skills like how to identify the main idea. With reciprocal teaching, the strategies students learn are in the service of a larger purpose: to understand what they are and to develop the critical ability to read to learn.

The second factor that we think is critical for the success of reciprocal teaching is that the teacher models expert strategies in a shared problem context of knowing that they will soon undertake the same task. After they have tried to do it themselves, and perhaps had difficulties, they listen with new knowledge about the task. That is, they can compare their own questions or summaries generated by the group. They can reflect on any differences, trying to understand what led to those differences. We have argued elsewhere that this kind of reflection is critical to learning (Collins and Brown, 1988).

Third, the technique of providing scaffolding is crucial in the success of reciprocal teaching for several reasons. Most importantly, it decomposes the task as necessary for the students to carry it out, thereby helping them to see how, in detail, to go about it. For example, in formulating questions, the teacher might want to see if the student can generate a question on his or her own; if not, she might suggest starting with a Why question about the agent in the story. If that fails, she might generate one herself and ask the student to reformulate it in his or her own words. In this way, it gets students started in the new skills, giving them a feel for the skills and helping them develop confidence that they can do them. With successful scaffolding techniques, students get as much support as they need to carry out the task, but no more. Hints and modelling are then gradually faded out, with students taking on more and more of the task as they become more skilful. These techniques of scaffolding and fading slowly build students confidence that they can master the skills required.

The final aspect of reciprocal teaching that we think is critical is having students assume the dual roles of producer and critic. They not only must produce good questions and summaries, but they also learn to evaluate the summaries or questions of others. By becoming critics as well as producers, students are forced to articulate their knowledge about what makes a good question, prediction, or summary. This knowledge then becomes more readily available for application to their own summaries and questions, thus improving a crucial aspect of their metacognitive skills. Moreover, once articulated, this knowledge can no longer simply reside in tacit form. It becomes more available for performing a variety of tasks; that is, it is freed from its contextual binding and can be used in many different contexts.

Writing

Scardamalia and Bereiter (1985; Scardamalia, Bereiter, and Steinbach, 1984) have developed an approach to the teaching of writing that relies on elements of cognitive apprenticeship. Based on contrasting models of novice and expert writing strategies, the approach provides explicit procedural supports, in the form of prompts, that are aimed at helping students adopt more sophisticated writing strategies. Like other exemplars of cognitive apprenticeship, their approach is designed to give students a grasp of the complex activities involved in expertise by explicit modeling of expert processes, gradually reduced support or scaffolding for students attempting to engage in the processes, and opportunities for reflection on their own and others' efforts.

According to Bereiter and Scardamalia (1987), children who are novices in writing use a 'knowledge telling' strategy. When given a topic to write on, they immediately produce text by writing their first idea, then their next idea, and so on, until they run out of ideas, at which point they stop. This very simple control strategy finesses most of the difficulties in composing. In contrast, experts spend time not only writing but also planning what they are going to write and revising what they have written (Hayes and Flower, 1980). As a result, they engage in a process that Scardamalia and Bereiter call 'knowledge transforming,' which incorporates the linear generation of text but is organized around a more complex structure of goal setting and problem-solving.

To encourage students to adopt a more sophisticated writing strategy, Scardamalia and Bereiter have developed a detailed cognitive analysis of the activities of expert writers. This analysis provides the basis for a set of prompts, *procedural facilitations* that are designed to reduce students' information-processing burden by allowing them to select from a limited number of diagnostic statements. For example, planning is broken down into five general processes or goals: (a) generating a new idea, (b) improving an idea, (c) elaborating on an idea, (d) identifying goals, and (e) putting ideas into a cohesive whole. For each process, they have developed a number of specific prompts, designed to aid students in their planning, as shown below. These prompts, which are akin to the suggestions made by the teacher in reciprocal teaching, serve to simplify the complex process of elaborating on one's plans by suggesting specific lines of thinking for students to follow. A set of prompts has been developed for the revision process as well (Scardamalia and Bereiter, 1983, 1985).

PLANNING CUES FOR OPINION ESSAYS
(From Scardamalia et al., 1984)

NEW IDEA

An even better idea is…

An important point I haven't considered yet is…

A better argument would be…

A different aspect would be…

A whole new way to think of this topic is…

No one will have thought of…

IMPROVE

I'm not being very clear about what I just said so…

I could make my main point clearer…

A criticism I should deal with in my paper is…

I really think this isn't necessary because…

I'm getting off the topic so…

This isn't very convincing because…

But many readers won't agree that…

To liven this up I'll…

ELABORATE

An example of this…

This is true, but it's not sufficient so…

My own feelings about this are…

I'll change this a little by…

The reason I think so…

Another reason that's good…

I could develop this idea by adding…

Another way to put it would be…

A good point on the other side of the argument is…

GOALS

A goal I think I could write to…

My purpose…

PUTTING IT TOGETHER

- If I want to start off with my strongest idea, I'll…

- I can tie this together by…

- My main point is…

Scardamalia and Bereiter's teaching method, like reciprocal teaching, proceeds through a combination of modeling, coaching, scaffolding, and fading. First, the teacher models how to use the prompts, which are written on cue cards, in generating ideas about a topic she is going to write on. The example below illustrates the kind of modeling done by a teacher during an early phase of instruction. Then the students each try to plan an essay on a new topic using the cue cards, a process the students call 'soloing.' While each student practices soloing, the teacher as well as other students evaluate the soloist's performance, by, for example, noticing discrepancies between the soloist's stated goals (e.g., to get readers to appreciate the difficulties of modern dance) and their proposed plans (to describe different kinds of dance). Students also become involved in discussing how to resolve problems that the soloist could not solve. As in the reciprocal teaching method, assumption of the role either of critic or producer is incremental, with students taking over more and more of the monitoring and problem-solving process from the teacher as their skills improve. Moreover, as the students internalize the processes invoked by the prompts, the cue cards are gradually faded out as well.

A TEACHER MODELS GETTING STARTED

ASSIGNMENT
(Suggested by students)
Write an essay on the topic 'Today's Rock Stars Are More Talented than Musicians of Long Ago.'

THINKING-ALOUD EXCERPT
I don't know a thing about modern rock stars. I can't think of the name of even one rock star. How about, David Bowie or Mick Jagger…But many readers won't agree that they are modern rock stars. I think they're both as old as I am. Let's see, my own feelings about this are … that I doubt if today's rock stars are more talented than ever. Anyhow, how would I know? I can't argue this… I need a new idea…An important point I haven't considered yet is…ah…well…what do we mean by talent? Am I talking about musical talent or ability to entertain – to do acrobatics? Hey, I may have a way into this topic. I could develop this idea by…

Note: Underlined phrases represent selection from planning cues similar to those shown in the outline for opinion essays.

Scardamalia and Bereiter have tested the effects of their approach on both the initial planning and the revision of student compositions. In a series of studies (Bereiter and Scardamalia, 1987), procedural facilitations were developed to help elementary school students evaluate, diagnose, and decide on revisions for their compositions. Results showed that each type of support was effective, independent of the other supports. And when all the facilitations were combined, they resulted in superior revisions for nearly every student and a tenfold increase in the frequency of idea-level revisions, without any decrease in stylistic revisions. Another study (Scardamalia et al., 1984) investigated the use of procedural cues to facilitate planning. Students gave the teacher assignments, often ones thought to be difficult for her. She used cues like those shown above to facilitate planning, modeling the process of using the cues to stimulate her thinking about the assignment. Pre- and post-comparisons of think-aloud protocols showed significantly more reflective activity on the part of experimental-group students, even when prompts were no longer available to them. Time spent in planning increased tenfold. And when students were given unrestricted time to plan, the texts of experimental-group students were judged significantly superior in thought content.

Clearly, Scardamalia and Bereiter's methods bring about significant changes in the nature and quality of student writing. In addition to the methods already discussed, we believe that there are two key reasons for their success. First, as in the reciprocal teaching approach to reading, their methods help students build a new conception of the writing process. Students initially consider writing to be a linear process of knowledge telling. By explicitly modeling and scaffolding expert processes, they are providing students with a new model of writing that involves planning and revising. Most students found this view of writing entirely new and showed it in their comments ('I don't usually ask myself those questions,' 'I never thought closely about what I wrote,' and 'They helped me look over the sentence, which I don't usually do.'). Moreover, because students rarely, if ever, see writers at work, they tend to hold naive beliefs about the nature of expert writing, thinking that writing is a smooth and easy process for 'good' writers. Live modeling helps to convey that this is not the case. The model demonstrates struggles, false starts, discouragement, and the like.

Second, because writing is a complex task, a key component of expertise are the control strategies by which the writer organizes the numerous lines of thinking involved in producing high-quality text. A clear need of student writers, therefore, is to develop more useful control strategies than evidenced in 'knowledge telling.' Scardamalia and Bereiter's methods encourage this development in an interesting way: the cue cards act to externalize not only the basic processes involved in planning but also to help students to keep track of the higher order intentions (such as generating an idea, elaborating or improving on an idea, and so on) that organize these basic processes.

Mathematical problem-solving[1]

Our third example is Schoenfeld's (1983, 1985) method for teaching mathematical problem-solving to college students. Like the other two, this method is based on a new analysis of the knowledge and processes required for expertise, where expertise is understood as the ability to carry out complex problem-solving tasks. And like the other two, this method incorporates the basic elements of a cognitive apprenticeship, using the methods of modeling, coaching, and fading

---

1. For those of you for whom it has been a while since you grappled with college math, let us assure you that you need not follow the substance of the math in this example in order to understand and appreciate what Schoenfeld is doing pedagogically when be brings to the surface reasoning processes that are normally covert.

and of encouraging student reflection on their own problem-solving processes. In addition, Schoenfeld's work introduces some new concerns, leading the way toward articulation of a more general framework for the development and evaluation of ideal learning environments.

One distinction between novices and experts in mathematics is that experts employ heuristic methods, usually acquired tacitly through long experience, to facilitate their problem-solving. To teach these methods directly, Schoenfeld formulated a set of heuristic strategies, derived from the problem-solving heuristics of Polya (1945). These *heuristic strategies* consist of rules of thumb for how to approach a given problem. One such heuristic specifies how to distinguish special cases in solving math problems: for example, for series problems in which there is an integer parameter in the problem statement, one should try the cases n = 1,2,3,4, and try to make an induction on those cases; for geometry problems, one should first examine cases with minimal complexity, such as regular polygons and right triangles. Schoenfeld taught a number of these heuristics and how to apply them in different kinds of math problems. In his experiments, Schoenfeld found that learning these strategies significantly increased students' problem-solving abilities.

But as he studied students' problem-solving further, he became aware of other critical factors affecting their skill, in particular what he calls control strategies. In Schoenfeld's analysis, *control strategies* are concerned with executive decisions, such as generating alternative courses of action, evaluating which will get you closer to a solution, evaluating which you are most likely to be able to carry out, considering what heuristics might apply, evaluating whether you are making progress toward a solution, and so on. Schoenfeld found that it was critical to teach control strategies, as well as heuristics.

As with the reading and writing examples, explicit teaching of these elements of expert practice yields a fundamentally new understanding of the domain for students. To students, learning mathematics had meant learning a set of mathematical operations and methods. Schoenfeld's method is teaching students that doing mathematics consists not only in applying problem-solving procedures but in reasoning about and managing problems using heuristics and control strategies.

Schoenfeld's teaching employs the elements of modeling, coaching, scaffolding, and fading in a variety of activities designed to highlight different aspects of the cognitive processes and knowledge structures required for expertise. For example, as a way of introducing new heuristics, he models their selection and use in solving problems for which they are particularly relevant. In this way, he exhibits the thinking processes (heuristics and control strategies) that go on in expert problem-solving but focuses student observation on the use and management of specific heuristics.

A MATHEMATICIAN THINKS OUT LOUD
(from Schoenfeld, 1983)

Problem

Let $P(x)$ and $Q(x)$ be two polynomials with 'reversed' coefficients:

$$P(x) = a_n x^n + a_{n-1} x^{n-1} + \ldots + a_2 x^2 + a_1 x + a_0,$$

$$Q(x) = a_0 x^n + a_1 x^{n-1} + \ldots + a_{n-2} x^2 + a_{n-1} x + a_n,$$

where $a_n \neq 0 \neq a_0$. What is the relationship between the roots of $P(x)$ and those of $Q(x)$? Prove your answer.

Expert Model

What do you do when you face a problem like this? I have no general procedure for finding the roots of a polynomial, much less for comparing the roots of two of them. Probably the best thing to do for the time being is to look at some simple examples and hope I can develop some intuition from them. Instead of looking at a pair of arbitrary polynomials, maybe I should look at a pair of quadratics: at least I can solve those. So, what happens if

$$P(x) = ax^2 + bx + c$$

and

$$Q(x) = cx^2 + bx + a?$$

The roots are

$$\frac{-b \pm \sqrt{b^2 - 4ac}}{2a}$$

$$\frac{-b \pm \sqrt{b^2 - 4ac}}{2c}$$

respectively.

That's certainly suggestive, because they have the same numerator, but I don't really see anything that I can push or that'll generalize. I'll give this a minute or two, but I may have to try something else....

Well, just for the record, let me look at the linear case. If $P(x) = ax + b$ and $Q(x) = bx + a$, the roots are b/a and a/b respectively.

They're reciprocals, but that's not too interesting in itself. Let me go back to quadratics. I still don't have much of a feel for what's going on. I'll do a couple of easy examples, and look for some sort of a pattern. The clever thing to do may be to pick polynomials I can factor; that way it'll be easy to keep track of the roots. All right, how about something easy like $(x + 2)(x + 3)$?

Then $P(x) = x^2 + 5x + 6$, with roots -2 and -3. So,
$Q(x) = 6x^2 + 5x + I = (2x + 1)(3x + 1)$, with roots $-1/2$ and $-1/3$.

Those are reciprocals too. Now that's interesting.

How about $P(x) = (3x + 5)(2x - 7) = 6x^2 - 11x - 35$? Its roots are $-5/3$ and $7/2$; $Q(x) = -35x^2 - 11x + 6 = -(35x^2 + 11x - 6) = -(7x - 2)(5x + 3)$.

All right, the roots are $2/7$ and $-3/5$. They're reciprocals again, and this time it can't be an accident. Better yet, took at the factors: they're reversed! What about

$P(x) (ax + b)(cx + d) = acx^2 + (bc + ad)x + bd$? Then
$Q(x) bdx^2 + (ad + bc)x + ac = (bx + a)(dx + c)$.

Aha! It works again, and I think this will generalize...

At this point there are two ways to go. I hypothesize that the roots of $P(x)$ are the reciprocals of the roots of $Q(x)$, in general. (If I'm not yet sure, I should try a factorable cubic or two.) Now, I can try to generalize the argument above, but it's not all that straightforward; not every polynomial can be factored, and keeping track of the coefficients may not be that easy.

It may be worth stopping, re-phrasing my conjecture, and trying it from scratch:

Let $P(x)$ and $Q(x)$ be two polynomials with 'reversed' coefficients. Prove that the roots of $P(x)$ and $Q(x)$ are reciprocals.

All right, let's take a look at what the problem asks for. What does it mean for some number, say r, to be a root of $P(x)$? It means that $P(r) = 0$. Now the conjecture says that the reciprocal of r is supposed to be a root to $Q(x)$. That says that $Q(1/r) = 0$. Strange. Let me go back to the quadratic case, and see what happens.

Let $P(x) = ax^2 + bx + c$, and $Q(x) = cx^2 + bx + a$. If r is a root of $P(x)$, then $P(r) = ar^2 + br + c = 0$. Now what does $Q(1/r)$ look like?

$$Q(1/r) = c(1/r)^2 + b(1/r) + a = \frac{c + br + ar^2}{r^2} = \frac{P(r)}{r^2} = 0$$

So it works, and this argument will generalize. Now I can write up a proof.

Proof

Let r be a root of $P(x)$, so that $P(r) = 0$. Observe that $r \neq 0$, since $a_0 \neq 0$. Further,

$$Q(1/r) = a_0(1/r)^n + a_1(1/r)^{n-1} + \ldots + a_{n-2}(1/r) + a_n = (1/r^n)(a_0 + a_1 r + a_2 r^2 + \ldots + a_{n-2}r^{n-2} + a_{n-1}r^{n-1} + a_n r^n) = (1/r^n)P(r) = 0,$$ so that $(1/r)$ is a root of $Q(x)$.

Conversely, if s is a root of $Q(x)$, we see that $P(1/s) = 0$. Q.E.D.

All right, now it's time for a postmortem. Observe that the proof, like a classical mathematical argument, is quite terse and presents the results of a thought process. But where did the inspiration for the proof come from? If you go back over the way that the argument evolved, you'll see there were two major breakthroughs.

The first had to do with understanding the problem, with getting a feel for it. The problem statement, in its full generality, offered little in the way of assistance. What we did was to *examine special cases* in order to look for a pattern. More specifically, our first attempt at special cases-looking at the quadratic formula didn't provide much insight. We had to get even more specific, as follows: *Look at a series of straightforward examples that are easy to calculate, in order to see if some sort of pattern emerges. With luck, you might be able to generalize the pattern.* In this case, we were looking for roots of polynomials, so we chose easily factorable ones. Obviously, different circumstances will lead to different choices. But that strategy allowed us to make a conjecture.

The second breakthrough came after we made the conjecture. Although we had some idea of why it ought to be true, the argument looked messy, and we stopped to reconsider for a while. What we did at that point was important, and is often overlooked: *we went back to the conditions of the*

> problem, explored them, and looked for tangible connections between them and the results we wanted. Questions like 'What does it mean for r to be a root of P(x)?', 'What does the reciprocal of r look like?' and 'What does it mean for (1/r) to be a root of Q(x)?' may seem almost trivial in isolation, but they focused our attention on the very things that gave us a solution.

Next, he gives the class problems to solve that lend themselves to the use of the heuristics he has introduced. During this collective problem-solving, he acts as a moderator, soliciting heuristics and solution techniques from the students while modeling the various control strategies for making judgments about how best to proceed. This division of labor has several effects. First, he turns over some of the problem-solving process to students by having them generate alternative courses of action but provides major support or scaffolding by managing the decisions about which course to pursue, when to change course, etc. Second, significantly, he no longer models the entire expert problem-solving process but a portion of it. In this way, he shifts the focus from the application or use of specific heuristics to the application or use of control strategies in managing those heuristics.

Like Scardamalia and Bereiter, Schoenfeld employs a third kind of modeling that is designed to change students' assumptions about the nature of expert problem-solving. He challenges students to find difficult problems and at the beginning of each class offers to try to solve one of their problems. Occasionally, the problems are hard enough that the students see him flounder in the face of real difficulties. During these sessions, he models for students not only the use of heuristics and control strategies but the fact that one's strategies sometimes fail. In contrast, textbook solutions and classroom demonstrations generally illustrate only the successful solution path, not the search space that contains all of the deadend attempts. Such solutions reveal neither the exploration in searching for a good method nor the necessary evaluation of the exploration. Seeing how experts deal with problems that are difficult for them is critical to students' developing a belief in their own capabilities. Even experts stumble, flounder, and abandon their search for a solution until another time. Witnessing these struggles helps students realize that thrashing is neither unique to them nor a sign of incompetence.

In addition to class demonstrations and collective problem-solving, Schoenfeld has students participate in small-group problem-solving sessions. During these sessions, Schoenfeld acts as a 'consultant' to make sure that the groups are proceeding in a reasonable fashion. Typically he asks three questions: what are they doing, why are they doing it, and how will success in what they are doing help them find a solution to the problem? Asking these questions serves two purposes: first, it encourages the students to reflect on their activities, thus promoting the development of general self-monitoring and diagnostic skills; second, it encourages them to articulate the reasoning behind their choices as they exercise control strategies. Gradually, the students, in anticipating his questioning, come to ask the questions of themselves, thus gaining control over reflective and metacognitive processes in their problem-solving. In these sessions, then, he is fading relative to both helping students generate heuristics and, ultimately, to exercising control over the process. In this way, they gradually gain control over the entire problem-solving process.

Schoenfeld (1983) advocates small-group problem-solving for several reasons. First, it gives the teacher a chance to coach students while they are engaged in semi-independent problem-solving; he cannot really coach them effectively on homework problems or class problems. Second, the necessity for group decision making in choosing among alternative solution methods provokes articulation, through discussion and argumentation, of the issues involved in exercising control processes. Such discussion encourages the development of the metacognitive skiffs involved, for example, monitoring and evaluating one's progress. Third, students get little opportunity in school to engage in collaborative efforts; group problem-solving gives them practice in the kind of collaboration prevalent in real-world problem-solving. Fourth, students are often insecure about their abilities, especially if they have difficulties with the problems. Seeing other students struggle alleviates some of this insecurity as students realize that difficulties in understanding are not unique to them, thus contributing to an enhancement of their beliefs about self, relative to others.

We believe that there is another important reason that small-group problem-solving is useful for learning: the differentiation and externalization of the roles and activities involved in solving complex problems. Successful problem-solving requires that one assume at least three different, though interrelated, roles at different points in the problem-solving process: that of moderator or executive, that of generator of alternative paths, and that of critic of alternatives. Small-group problem-solving differentiates and externalizes these roles: different people naturally take on different roles, and problem-solving proceeds along these lines. And here, as in reciprocal teaching, students may play different roles, so that they gain practice in all the activities they need to internalize.

There is one final aspect of Schoenfeld's method that we think is critical and that is different from the other methods we have discussed: what he calls postmortem analysis. As with other aspects of Schoenfeld's method, students alternate with the teacher in producing postmortem analyses. First, after modeling the problem-solving process for a given problem, Schoenfeld recounts the solution method, highlighting those features of the process that can be generalized. For example, he might note the heuristics that were employed, the points in the solution process where he or the class engaged in generating alternatives, the reasons for the decision to pursue one alternative before another, and so on. In short, he provides what Collins and Brown (1988) have labeled an abstracted replay, that is, a recapitulation of some process designed to focus students' attention on the critical decisions or actions. Postmortem analysis also occurs when individual students explain the process by which they solved their homework problems. Here students are required to generate an abstracted replay of their own problem-solving process, as the basis for a class critique of their methods. The alternation between expert and student postmortem analyses enables the class to compare student problem-solving processes and strategies with those of the expert; such comparisons provide the basis for diagnosing student difficulties and for making incremental adjustments in student performance.

A FRAMEWORK FOR DESIGNING LEARNING ENVIRONMENTS

Our discussion of cognitive apprenticeship raises numerous pedagogical and theoretical issues that we believe are important to the design of learning environments generally. To facilitate consideration of these issues, we have developed a framework consisting of four dimensions that constitute any learning environment: content, method, sequence, and sociology. Relevant to each of these dimensions is a set of characteristics that we believe should be considered in constructing or evaluating learning environments. These characteristics are described in detail below, with examples from reading, writing, and mathematics.

Content

Recent cognitive research has begun to differentiate the types of knowledge required for expertise. In particular, researchers have begun to distinguish among the concepts, facts, and procedures associated with expertise and various types of strategic knowledge. We use the term strategic knowledge to refer to the usually tacit knowledge that underlies an expert's ability to make use of concepts, facts, and procedures as necessary to solve problems and accomplish tasks. This sort of expert problem-solving knowledge involves problem-solving heuristics (or 'rules of thumb') and the strategies that control the problem-solving process. Another type of strategic knowledge, often overlooked, includes the learning strategies that experts use to acquire new concepts, facts, and procedures in their own or another field.

We should emphasize that much of experts' strategic knowledge depends on their knowledge of facts, concepts, and procedures. For instance, in the math example discussed earlier, Schoenfeld's students could not begin to apply the strategies he is teaching if they did not have a solid grounding in mathematical knowledge.

1. ***Domain knowledge*** includes the concepts, facts, and procedures explicitly identified with a particular subject matter; these are generally explicated in school textbooks, class lectures, and demonstrations. This kind of knowledge, although certainly important, provides insufficient clues for many students about how to solve problems and accomplish tasks in a domain. Moreover, when it is learned in isolation from realistic problem contexts and expert problem-solving practices, domain knowledge tends to remain inert in situations for which it is appropriate, even for successful students. And finally, although at least some concepts can be formally described, many of the crucial subtleties of their meaning are best acquired through applying them in a variety of problem situations. Indeed, it is only through encountering them in real problem-solving that most students will learn the boundary conditions and entailments of much of their domain knowledge. Examples of domain knowledge in reading are vocabulary, syntax, and phonics rules.

2. ***Heuristic strategies*** are generally effective techniques and approaches for accomplishing tasks that might be regarded as 'tricks of the trade'; they don't always work, but when they do, they are quite helpful. Most heuristics are tacitly acquired by experts through the practice of solving problems; however, there have been noteworthy attempts to address heuristic learning explicitly (Schoenfeld, 1985). For example, a standard heuristic for writing is to plan to rewrite the introduction and, therefore, to spend relatively little time crafting it in the first draft. In mathematics, a heuristic for solving problems is to try to find a solution for simple cases and see if the solution generalizes.

3. ***Control strategies***, as the name suggests, control the process of carrying out a task. These are sometimes referred to as 'metacognitive' strategies (Palincsar and Brown, 1984; Schoenfeld, 1985). As students acquire more and more heuristics for solving problems, they encounter a new management or control problem: how to select among the possible problem-solving strategies, how to decide when to change strategies, and so on. Control strategies have monitoring, diagnostic, and remedial components; decisions about how to proceed in a task

generally depend on an assessment of one's current state relative to one's goals, on an analysis of current difficulties, and on the strategies available for dealing with difficulties. For example, a comprehension-monitoring strategy might be to try to state the main point of a section one has just read; if one cannot do so, then one has not understood the text, and it might be best to reread parts of the text. In mathematics, a simple control strategy for solving a complex problem might be to switch to a new part of a problem if one is stuck.

4. *Learning strategies* are strategies for learning any of the other kinds of content described above. Knowledge about how to learn ranges from general strategies for exploring a new domain to more specific strategies for extending or reconfiguring knowledge in solving problems or carrying out complex tasks. For example, if students want to learn to solve problems better, they need to learn how to relate each step in the example problems worked in textbooks to the principles discussed in the text (Chi et al., 1989). If students want to write better, they need to find people to read their writing who can give helpful critiques and explain the reasoning underlying the critiques (most people cannot). They also need to learn to analyze other's texts for strengths and weaknesses.

Method

Teaching methods should be designed to give students the opportunity to observe, engage in, and invent or discover expert strategies in context. Such an approach will enable students to see how these strategies combine with their factual and conceptual knowledge and how they use a variety of resources in the social and physical environment. The six teaching methods advocated here fall roughly into three groups: the first three (modeling, coaching, and scaffolding) are the core of cognitive apprenticeship, designed to help students acquire an integrated set of skills through processes of observation and guided practice. The next two (articulation and reflection) are methods designed to help students both to focus their observations of expert problem-solving and to gain conscious access to (and control of) their own problem-solving strategies. The final method (exploration) is aimed at encouraging learner autonomy, not only in carrying out expert problem-solving processes but also in defining or formulating the problems to be solved.

1. *Modeling* involves an expert's performing a task so that the students can observe and build a conceptual model of the processes that are required to accomplish it. In cognitive domains, this requires the externalization of usually internal processes and activities – specifically, the heuristics and control processes by which experts apply their basic conceptual and procedural knowledge. For example, a teacher might model the reading process by reading

aloud in one voice, while verbalizing her thought processes in another voice (Collins and Smith, 1982). In mathematics, as described above, Schoenfeld models the process of solving problems by having students bring difficult new problems for him to solve in class.

2. *Coaching* consists of observing students while they carry out a task and offering hints, scaffolding, feedback, modeling, reminders, and new tasks aimed at bringing their performance closer to expert performance. Coaching may serve to direct students' attention to a previously unnoticed aspect of the task or simply to remind the student of some aspect of the task that is known but has been temporarily overlooked. The content of the coaching interaction is immediately related to specific events or problems that arise as the student attempts to accomplish the target task. In Palincsar and Brown's reciprocal teaching of reading, the teacher coaches students while they ask questions, clarify their difficulties, generate summaries, and make predictions.

3. *Scaffolding* refers to the supports the teacher provides to help the student carry out the task. These supports can take either the forms of suggestions or help, as in reciprocal teaching, or they can take the form of physical supports, as with the cue cards used by Scardamalia, Bereiter, and Steinbach to facilitate writing, or the short skis used to teach downhill skiing (Burton, Brown, and Fisher, 1984). When scaffolding is provided by a teacher, it involves the teacher in executing parts of the task that the student cannot yet manage. A requisite to such scaffolding is accurate diagnosis of the student's current skill level or difficulty and the availability of an intermediate step at the appropriate level of difficulty in carrying out the target activity. Fading involves the gradual removal of supports until students are on their own.

4. *Articulation* involves any method of getting students to articulate their knowledge, reasoning, or problem-solving processes. We have identified several different methods of articulation. First, inquiry teaching (Collins and Stevens, 1982, 1983) is a strategy of questioning students to lead them to articulate and refine their understanding of concepts and procedures in different domains. For example, an inquiry teacher in reading might systematically question students about why one summary of the text is good but another is poor, to get the students to formulate an explicit model of a good summary. Second, teachers might encourage students to articulate their thoughts as they carry out their problem-solving, as do Scardamalia et al. Third, they might have students assume the critic or monitor role in cooperative activities, as do all three models we discussed, and thereby lead students to formulate and articulate their ideas to other students.

5. *Reflection* involves enabling students to compare their own problem-solving processes with those of an expert, another student, and ultimately, an internal cognitive model of expertise. Reflection is enhanced by the use of various techniques for reproducing or 'replaying' the performances of both expert and novice for comparison. The level of detail for a replay may vary depending on the student's stage of learning, but usually some form of 'abstracted replay,' in which the critical features of expert and student performance are highlighted, is desirable (Collins and Brown, 1988). For reading or writing, methods to encourage reflection might consist of recording students as they think out loud and then replaying the tape for comparison with the thinking of experts and other students.

6. *Exploration* involves pushing students into a mode of problem-solving on their own. Forcing them to do exploration is critical, if they are to learn how to frame questions or problems that are interesting and that they can solve. Exploration is the natural culmination of the fading of supports. It involves not only fading in problem-solving but fading in problem setting as well. But students do not know a *priori* how to explore a domain productively. So exploration strategies need to be taught as part of learning strategies more generally. Exploration as a method of teaching involves setting general goals for students and then encouraging them to focus on particular subgoals of interest to them, or even to revise the general goals as they come upon something more interesting to pursue. For example, in reading, the teacher might send the students to the library to investigate theories about why the stock market crashed in 1929. In writing, students might be encouraged to write an essay defending the most outrageous thesis they can devise. In mathematics, students might be asked to generate and test hypotheses about teenage behavior given a database on teenagers detailing their backgrounds and how they spend their time and money.

Sequencing

In sequencing activities for students, it is important to give students tasks that structure their learning but that preserve the meaningfulness of what they are doing. This leads us to three principles that must be balanced in sequencing activities for students.

1. *Global before local skills*. In tailoring (Lave, 1988), apprentices learn to put together a garment from precut pieces before learning to cut out the pieces themselves. The chief effect of this sequencing principle is to allow students to build a conceptual map, so to speak, before attending to the details of the terrain (Norman, 1973). In general, having students build a conceptual model

of the target skill or process (which is also encouraged by expert modeling) accomplishes two things: first, even when the learner is able to accomplish only a portion of a task, having a clear conceptual model of the overall activity helps him make sense of the portion that he is carrying out. Second, the presence of a clear conceptual model of the target task acts as a guide for the learner's performance, thus improving his ability to monitor his own progress and to develop attendant self-correction skills. This principle requires some form of scaffolding. In algebra, for example, students may be relieved of having to carry out low-level computations in which they lack skill in order to concentrate on the higher-order reasoning and strategies required to solve an interesting problem (Brown, 1985).

2. *Increasing complexity* refers to the construction of a sequence of tasks such that more and more of the skills and concepts necessary for expert performance are required (VanLehn and Brown, 1980; Burton, Brown, and Fisher, 1984; White, 1984). For example, in the tailoring apprenticeship described by Lave, apprentices first learn to construct drawers, which have straight lines, few pieces, and no special features, such as waistbands or pockets. They then learn to construct blouses, which require curved lines, patch pockets, and the integration of a complex subpiece, the collar. There are two mechanisms for helping students manage increasing complexity. The first mechanism is to sequence tasks in order to control task complexity. The second key mechanism is the use of scaffolding, which enables students to handle at the outset, with the support of the teacher or other helper, the complex set of activities needed to accomplish any interesting task. For example, in reading, increasing task complexity might consist of progressing from relatively short texts, employing straightforward syntax and concrete description, to texts in which complex interrelated ideas and the use of abstractions make interpretation difficult.

3. *Increasing diversity* refers to the construction of a sequence of tasks in which a wider and wider variety of strategies or skills are required. Although it is important to practice a new strategy or skill repeatedly in a sequence of (increasingly complex) tasks, as a skill becomes well learned, it becomes increasingly important that tasks requiring a diversity of skills and strategies be introduced so that the student learns to distinguish the conditions under which they do (and do not) apply. Moreover, as students learn to apply skiffs to more diverse problems, their strategies acquire a richer net of contextual associations and thus are more readily available for use with unfamiliar or novel problems. For reading, task diversity might be attained by mixing reading for pleasure, reading for memory (studying), and reading to find out some particular information in the context of some other task.

160

Sociology

The final dimension in our framework concerns the sociology of the learning environment. For example, tailoring apprentices learn their craft not in a special, segregated learning environment but in a busy tailoring shop. They are surrounded both by masters and other apprentices, all engaged in the target skills at varying levels of expertise. And they are expected, from the beginning, to engage in activities that contribute directly to the production of actual garments, advancing quickly toward independent, skilled production. As a result, apprentices learn skills in the context of their application to realistic problems, within a culture focused on and defined by expert practice. Furthermore, certain aspects of the social organization of apprenticeship encourage productive beliefs about the nature of learning and of expertise that are significant to learners' motivation, confidence, and most importantly, their orientation toward problems that they encounter as they learn. From our consideration of these general issues, we have abstracted critical characteristics affecting the sociology of learning.

1. *Situated learning:* A critical element of fostering learning is to have students carry out tasks and solve problems in an environment that reflects the multiple uses to which their knowledge will be put in the future. Situated learning serves several different purposes. First, students come to understand the purposes or uses of the knowledge they are learning. Second, they learn by actively using knowledge rather than passively receiving it. Third, they learn the different conditions under which their knowledge can be applied. As we pointed out in the discussion of Schoenfeld's work, students have to learn when to use a particular strategy and when not to use it (i.e., the application conditions of their knowledge). Fourth, learning in multiple contexts induces the abstraction of knowledge, so that students acquire knowledge in a dual form, both tied to the contexts of its uses and independent of any particular context. This unbinding of knowledge from a specific context fosters its transfer to new problems and new domains. For example, reading and writing instruction might be situated in the context of students putting together a book on what they learn about science. Dewey created a situated learning environment in his experimental school by having the students design and build a clubhouse (Cuban, 1984), a task that emphasizes arithmetic and planning skills.

2. *Community of practice* refers to the creation of a learning environment in which the participants actively communicate about and engage in the skills involved in expertise, where expertise is understood as the practice of solving problems and carrying out tasks in a domain. Such a community leads to a sense of ownership, characterized by personal investment and mutual

dependency. It can't be forced, but it can be fostered by common projects and shared experiences. Activities designed to engender a community of practice for reading might engage students and teacher in discussing how they interpret what they read and use those interpretations for a wide variety of purposes, including those that arise in other classes or domains.

3. *Intrinsic motivation:* Related to the issue of situated learning and the creation of a community of practice is the need to promote intrinsic motivation for learning. Lepper and Greene (1979) and Malone (1981) discuss the importance of creating learning environments in which students perform tasks because they are intrinsically related to an interesting or at least coherent goal, rather than for some extrinsic reason, like getting a good grade or pleasing the teacher. In reading and writing, for example, intrinsic motivation might be achieved by having students communicate with students in another part of the world by electronic mail (Collins, 1986; Levin, 1982).

4. *Exploiting cooperation* refers to having students work together in a way that fosters cooperative problem-solving. Learning through cooperative problem-solving is both a powerful motivator and a powerful mechanism for extending learning resources. In reading, activities to exploit cooperation might involve having students break up into pairs, where one student articulates his thinking process while reading and the other student questions the first student about why he made different inferences. Cooperation can be blended with competition; for example, individuals might work together in groups to compete with other groups.

PRINCIPLES FOR DESIGNING
COGNITIVE APPRENTICESHIP ENVIRONMENTS

CONTENT: types of knowledge required for expertise

- **Domain knowledge:** subject matter specific concepts, facts, and procedures

- **Heuristic strategies:** generally applicable techniques for accomplishing tasks

- **Control strategies:** general approaches for directing one's solution process

- **Learning strategies:** knowledge about how to learn new concepts, facts, and procedures

---

METHOD: ways to promote the development of expertise

- **Modeling:** teacher performs a task so students can observe

- **Coaching:** teacher observes and facilitates while students perform a task

- **Scaffolding:** teacher provides supports to help the student perform a task

- **Articulation:** teacher encourages students to verbalize their knowledge and thinking

- **Reflection:** teacher enables students to compare their performance with others

- **Exploration:** teacher invites students to pose and solve their own problems

SEQUENCING: keys to ordering learning activities

- **Global before local skills:** focus on conceptualizing the whole task before executing the parts

- **Increasing complexity:** meaningful tasks gradually increasing in difficulty

- **Increasing diversity:** practice in a variety of situations to emphasize broad application

SOCIOLOGY: social characteristics of learning environments

- **Situated learning:** students learn in the context of working on realistic tasks

- **Community of practice:** communication about different ways to accomplish meaningful tasks

- **Intrinsic motivation:** students set personal goals to seek skills and solutions

- **Cooperation:** students work together to accomplish their goals

CONCLUSION

Cognitive apprenticeship is not a model of teaching that gives teachers a packaged formula for instruction. Instead, it is an instructional paradigm for teaching. Cognitive apprenticeship is not a relevant model for all aspects of teaching. It does not make sense to use it to teach the rules of conjugation in French or to teach the elements of the periodic table. If the targeted goal of learning is a rote task, cognitive apprenticeship is not an appropriate model of instruction. Cognitive apprenticeship is a useful instructional paradigm when a teacher needs to teach a fairly complex task to students.

Cognitive apprenticeship does not require that the teacher permanently assume the role of the 'expert' – in fact, we would imagine that the opposite should happen. Teachers need to encourage students to explore questions teachers cannot answer, to challenge solutions the 'experts' have found – in short, to allow the role of 'expert' and 'student' to be transformed. Cognitive apprenticeship encourages the student to become the expert.

How might a teacher apply the ideas of cognitive apprenticeship in his or her classroom? We don't believe that there is a formula for implementing the activities of modeling, scaffolding and fading, and coaching. Ultimately, it is up to the teacher to identify ways in which cognitive apprenticeship can work in his or her own domain of teaching.

Apprenticeship is the way we learn most naturally. It characterized learning before there were schools, from learning one's language to learning how to run an empire. We have very successful models of how apprenticeship methods, in all their dimensions, can be applied to teaching the school curriculum of reading, writing, and mathematics. These models, and the framework we have developed, help point the way toward the redesign of schooling, so that students may better acquire true expertise and robust problem-solving skills, as well as an improved ability to learn throughout life.

ACKNOWLEDGMENTS

The work upon which this publication was based was supported in part by the Office of Educational Research and Improvement under Cooperative Agreement No. OEG 0087C 100 1, with the Reading Research and Education Center at the University of Illinois, Champaign-Urbana and Bolt Beranek and Newman Inc. It was also supported in part by the Institute for the Learning Sciences at Northwestern University, which was established in 1989 with the support of Andersen Consulting, part of The Arthur Andersen Worldwide Organization. The publication does not necessarily reflect the views of the agencies supporting the research. We thank Lauren Resnick for suggesting the writing of this paper, Susan Newman for her contributions to the original paper on cognitive apprenticeship, and Sharon Carver for developing the table summarizing the principles of cognitive apprenticeship.

REFERENCES

Bereiter, C., and Scardamalia, M. (1987). *The Psychology of Written Composition*. Hillsdale, NJ: Lawrence Erlbaum Associates.

Brown, J. S. (1985). 'Idea-amplifiers: New Kinds of Electronic Learning.' *Educational Horizons*, 63, 108–112.

Brown, J.S., Collins, A., and Duguid, P (1989). 'Situated Cognition and the Culture of Learning.' *Educational Researcher*, 18(1), 32–42.

Burton, R., Brown, J.S., and Fisher, G. (1984). 'Skiing as a Model of Instruction.' In B. Rogoff and J. Lave (Eds.), *Everyday Cognition: Its Development and Social Context*. Cambridge, MA: Harvard University Press.

Chi, M.T.H., Bassok, M., Lewis, M.W., Reimann, P., Glaser, R. (1989). 'Self-Explanations: How Students Study and Use Examples in Learning to Solve Problems.' *Cognitive Science*, 13, 145–182.

Collins, A. (1986). 'Teaching Reading and Writing with Personal Computers.' In J. Orasanu (Ed.), *A Decade of Reading Research: Implications for Practice*. Hillsdale, NJ: Erlbaum.

Collins, A., and Brown, J.S. (1988). 'The Computer as a Tool for Learning through Reflection.' In H. Mandl and A. Lesgold (Eds.), *Learning Issues for Intelligent Tutoring Systems* (pp. 1–18). New York: Springer-Verlag.

Collins, A., and Smith, E.E. (1982). 'Teaching the Process of Reading Comprehension.' In D.K. Detterman and R.J. Sternberg (Eds.), *How Much and How Can Intelligence Be Increased?* Norwood, NJ: Ablex.

Collins, A., and Stevens, A.L. (1982). 'Goals and Strategies of Inquiry Teachers.' In R. Glaser (Ed.), *Advances in Instructional Psychology (Vol. 2)*. Hillsdale, NJ: Erlbaum.

Collins, A., and Stevens, A.L. (1983). 'A Cognitive Theory of Interactive Teaching.' In C.M. Reigeluth (Ed.), *Instructional Design Theories and Models: An Overview*. Hillsdale, NJ: Erlbaum.

Collins, A., Brown, J.S., and Newman, S.E. (1989). 'Cognitive Apprenticeship: Teaching the Craft of Reading, Writing and Mathematics!' In L.B. Resnick (ed.) *Knowing, Learning, and Instruction: Essa in Honor of Robert Glaser* Hillsdale, NJ: Erlbaum, and in Brown, J.S., Collins, A., and Duguid, P. (1989). 'Situated Cognition and the Culture of Learning.' Educational Researcher, 18 (1), 32–42.

Cuban, L. (1984), *How Teachers Taught*. New York: Longman.

Hayes J.R., and Flower, L. (1980). 'Identifying the Organization of Writing Processes.' In L.W Gregg and E.R. Steinberg (Eds.), *Cognitive Processes in Writing*. Hillsdale, NJ: Erlbaum.

Lave, J. (1988). 'The Culture of Acquisition and the Practice of Understanding.' (Report No. IRL88-0007). Palo-Alto, CA: Institute for Research on Learning.

Lave, J. and Wenger, E. (1991). *Situated Learning: Legitimate Peripheral Participation*. New York: Cambridge University Press.

Lepper, M.R. and Greene, D. (1979). *The Hidden Costs of Reward*. Hillsdale, NJ: Erlbaum.

Levin, J.A. (1982). 'Microcomputer Communication Networks for Education.' The Quarterly Newsletter of the Laboratory of Comparative Human Cognition 4, No. 2.

Malone, T. (1981). 'Toward a Theory of Intrinsically Motivating Instruction.' *Cognitive Science*, 4, 333–369.

Norman, D.A. (1973). 'Memory, Knowledge, and the Answering of Questions.' In R.L. Solso (Ed.), *Contemporary Issues in Cognitive Psychology The Loyola Symposium*. Washington, D.C.: Winston.

Palincsar, A.S. (1986). 'Metacognitive Strategy Instruction.' *Exceptional Children*, 53, 118–125.

Palincsar, A.S. (1987). 'Reciprocal Teaching.' *Instructor, XCVI No. 2*, 5–60.

Palincsar, A.S., and Brown, A. L. (1984). 'Reciprocal Teaching of Comprehension-fostering and Monitoring Activities.' *Cognition and Instruction*, 1, 117–175.

Polya, G. (1945). *How To Solve It*. Princeton, NJ: Princeton University Press.

Scardamalia, M., and Bereiter, C. (1983). 'The Development of Evaluative, Diagnostic and Remedial Capabilities in Children's Composing.' In M. Martlew (Ed.), *The Psychology of Written Language: A Developmental Approach* (pp. 67–95). London: Wiley.

Scardamalia. M., and Bereiter, C. (1985). 'Fostering the Development of Self-regulation in Children's Knowledge Processing.' In S.F. Chipman, J.W. Segal, and R. Glaser (Eds.), *Thinking and Learning Skills: Research and Open Questions*. Hillsdale, NJ: Lawrence Erlbaum Associates.

Scardamalia, M., and Bereiter, C., and Steinbach, R. (1984). 'Teachability of Reflective Process in Written Composition.' *Cognitive Science*, 8, 173–190.

Schoenfeld, A.H. (1983). 'problem-solving in the Mathematics Curriculum: A Report, Recommendations and an Annotated Bibliography.' The Mathematical Association of America, *MAA Notes*, No. 1.

Schoenfeld, A.H. (1985). *Mathematical problem-solving.* New York: Academic Press.

Van Lehn, K. and Brown, J.S. (1980). 'Planning Nets: A Representation for Formalizing Analogies and Semantic Models for Procedural Skills.' In R. E. Snow, PA. Federico, and WE. Montague (Eds.), *Aptitude Learning and Instruction, Vol. 2: Cognitive Process Analyses of Learning and Problem-Solving.* Hillsdale, NJ: Erlbaum.

White, B.Y. (1984). 'Designing Computer Games To Help Physics Students Understand Newton's Laws of Motion.' *Cognition and Instruction*, 1, 69–108.

CPSIA information can be obtained
at www.ICGtesting.com
Printed in the USA
LVHW050534090321
680926LV00003B/9